The Five Pillars of Leadership

—how to bridge the leadership gap

Paul J. Meyer and Randy Slechta

The 5 Pillars of Leadership
Second Edition

ISBN: 0-937539-90-2

LCCN: 2002101953

Published by
Executive Books
206 West Allen Street
Mechanicsburg, PA 17055

Printed in the United States of America

GEORGE BUSH

January 13, 1998

Dear Paul,

Let me take this opportunity to once again express my high regard for you
and for what you stand for.

You have motivated so many people in a most constructive way, thus
helping create a new generation of leaders.

On a very personal basis, I will always be grateful for your loyal support.

I hope your new book, *Bridging the Leadership Gap*, will motivate its
many readers. You are so well qualified to write on leadership.

Warmest regards,

Mr. Paul J. Meyer
Founder
Success Motivation Institute, Inc.
Post Office Box 2508
Waco, Texas 76702-2508

Letter written by former President, George Bush, to Paul J. Meyer in
regards to the first printing of *Bridging the Leadership Gap*, now titled
The Five Pillars of Leadership.

Endorsements

Here's a book that will enable you to become an empowered and empowering leader. Paul J. Meyer's powerful and proven techniques will guide you to tap and harness your God-given potential for effective leadership. By internalizing and practicing these strategies, you will achieve extraordinary success in every facet of your life and business.

Fr. Anthony A. D'Souza, S.J.
Director, Xavier Institute of Management
Bombay, India

This is a 'must-read' work from two outstanding entrepreneurs. This book will help any leader serious about achieving results through people. The processes in this book are invaluable for anyone who wants to achieve important personal and business goals.

Ruth Matheson, President
Leadership Skills, Inc.
Canada

Too many books focus on the trappings of leadership, not the essentials. These essentials can be learned and developed by following the advice of Paul Meyer. Those who possess leadership qualities can improve and augment those attributes by bridging the leadership gap.

David Sibley, State Senator
District 22, Texas

At the age of 25, Paul Meyer and SMI made a significant impact on my leadership development. This book will bridge the leadership gap for you.

Dr. John C. Maxwell, author and founder
INJOY, Inc.

This book is mandatory reading for anyone who is in a position of leadership, regardless of the level of responsibility. If your desire is to achieve maximum success and fulfillment from life, this book will help.

> *Kenneth H. Cooper, M.D., founder*
> *The Cooper Clinic*

Paul J. Meyer's principles transcend time and cultures. Since founding my company nearly 50 years ago, I have enjoyed well-earned success. I am greatly indebted to Mr. Meyer for my business growth. I highly recommend all of Mr. Meyer's programs and this exciting book.

> *Toshio Sumino, Founder and Chairman*
> *Autobacs Seven, Ltd.,*
> *Japan*

Africa is the richest continent in the world in terms of natural resources, but to release this wealth for the benefit of its people requires "The Five Pillars of Leadership" formulated in this book. It is the blueprint for successful management and leadership based on experience in over 60 countries since 1960. The leadership formulated so concisely in this book is a must-read for every leader on the African Continent.

> *Ian G. Dawson*
> *Master Licensee*
> *LMI – Southern Africa*

This book is an inspirational MUST READ for anyone wanting to make a leadership contribution to his or her family, organization, or community. The universal principles will work for anyone.

> *Grant Sexton*
> *Managing Director*
> *Leadership Management Australia*

Never before have we faced such an uncertain future. This book offers you deep insights to clarify your value system and understand the key ingredients of becoming a true leader, both in your professional and personal lives. A great book for those who want to turn uncertainties into opportunities!

William Cham
Master Licensee
SMI - Singapore

Paul J. Meyer has a genius for simplifying complex theory into clear, understandable and practical action steps. This book provides a pathway to greater leadership, success, and fulfillment in life.

Paul R. Brown, President and CEO
Leadership Dynamics, Inc.

In this book, Paul J. Meyer reveals the distilled essence of 50 years of meticulously chronicled leadership study and experience. He has lived it out. Here you read in clear, concise language the tried and proven steps for authentic leadership.

It's been said that the medium is the message. That's true in this case. Paul J. Meyer has demonstrated leadership in the establishment and overseeing more than 40 businesses in 60 nations.

I listened to a senior vice chairman of the Peoples Republic of China ply Meyer with questions. Meyer's modest but brilliant response must have impressed the vice chairman as much as it did me. The next day the Chinese newspapers carried the interview on the front page in detail. I observed Japanese and American leaders hanging on Meyer's every word at a reception hosted by former U. S. Ambassador to Japan, Mike Mansfield.

Meyer leads more by example than by precept though he possesses a rare ability to communicate. Since 1960, I have read everything—countless volumes—he has written.

In a day of growing consensus thinking that stifles leadership, Paul J. Meyer lays out in clear and compelling terms the formula for bridging the leadership gap.

John Edmund Haggai
Haggai Institute for Advanced Leadership Training
Singapore

Contents

Acknowledgements

Deepest appreciation to Dr. Barbara Chesser,
Tonette Holle, Jim Moore, and Vicki York.

Foreword by Drayton McLane

Leadership is a timeless river flowing endlessly toward the great vast tomorrow. Equally timeless is the need to shape and mold the river's channels. The effort to continually remanufacture leadership continues as men and women seek new ways to guide, manage, and motivate others.

This is as it should be—all of us should strive to improve our leadership mettle. The problem lies not with our desire to grow and become more than we already are, but rather in our tendency to readily accept, embrace, and apply flawed and simplistic solutions to vexing and complex problems.

In stark contrast, Paul J. Meyer and Randy Slechta have produced a new leadership and management creed—a methodology that is both practical and personal.

All successful organizations build upon three key strengths: an intimate knowledge of where the group intends to go and how it will get there, the ability of both leaders and team members to focus on a productive contribution to themselves and others, and the common desire to do whatever is necessary to achieve a positive outcome. A leadership gap is created whenever one or more of these three elements is neglected or underdeveloped.

To span that gap, Meyer and Slechta propose that we go back to the foundation of leadership: the 5 pillars of leadership. From this solid base, any and every leader can grow and excel.

Unlike the panacea presented by the quick-fix gurus, this leadership bridge cannot be constructed overnight. Several months, even years, will be required to implement fully the grand strategy brought forth in this book. Fortunately, leaders and team members can apply themselves to the long task, secure in the knowledge that the end result will be as they themselves have designed it.

In the final analysis, that is the collective genius at the root of this work. Whether we realize it or not, all of us design our own outcomes. Meyer and Slechta offer us a system for doing just that. They reaffirm our basic responsibility for success or failure, and reestablish us as the makers and molders of our own destiny.

Matters of business and personal development are far too important to be left to chance, and the quick-fixes that are legion in the marketplace have shown themselves to be little more than worthless.

What you hold in your hands is a unique new strategy for dealing with the age-old problem of leading and motivating others.

–Drayton McLane
Chairman, McLane Group
Past Vice Chairman, Wal-Mart

Chapter One

Where Effective
Leadership Begins

Never before in human history has society witnessed such a pressing demand for effective leadership. Today, proven leaders earn multi-million-dollar salaries at the head of giant corporations, revel in the power and prestige of high political office, and are at the forefront of new technological endeavors. But the current state of society demands even more of leaders—and requires that the quantity of leaders increase along with the quality of leadership they offer.

Over the past five or six decades, popular culture has undergone enormous change. Americans have witnessed their strongest social unit—the family—slowly disintegrate. What was once considered fringe behavior is now mainstream. As global citizens, we were led into difficult situations almost by default. Now that we are paying the price for dramatic, largely unplanned change, the demand for effective leadership is stronger than ever.

The hope is not that leadership can save us from ourselves and restore what was once right and proper, but rather determine where we want to go from here and how we intend to get there. Society can no longer afford to be surprised by the depth of social and political change. In decades to come, we will depend upon leaders at every level to chart a course toward a brighter, more positive world.

The lack of leadership

Is it fair to say that all the challenges we face today stem from a lack of effective leadership? Certainly not! Most, if not all, have resulted from our own choices. For good or bad, we made decisions that will continue to mold and shape our world for generations to come. We must accentuate the good decisions and find a way to reshape the bad. *That, in essence, is the challenge of effective leadership.*

It is obvious that some of our past leadership has not been particularly effective. Consider, for example, the collapse and/or massive downsizing of many large corporations where literally tens of thousands of workers are suddenly unemployed. While we cannot say that all the ills of the world would have passed us by had effective leadership been guiding society, it is not difficult to imagine that there might have been a better day.

The only real way to win over the trials we face is to meet those challenges with qualified, understanding, values-based leadership. Now is the time for all aspiring leaders to step into the arena and onto the field for their organization, for their society, and for their fellow man.

The stakes are incredibly high.

The only way out

Those who refuse to believe that effective leadership can rescue us from our self-imposed dilemmas face another question: "If leadership cannot help us solve our difficulties, what can?"

John F. Kennedy once noted, "Our problems are manmade...therefore, they can be solved by man." It stands to reason that many of today's problems—created at least partly by a lack of qualified, effective leadership—can be solved by the application of exactly the quality that has gone missing in our society. If man's problems are to be solved by man, effective leadership must lead the way.

Leaders hold in their hands the power to right social wrongs, point organizations toward success, and bring society back onto an even keel. They cradle the seed of opportunity for a global business renaissance and world political stability. Effective leaders carry with them the hopes and dreams of millions who wish only to become more than they are.

Effective leadership is indeed a noble pursuit. Anyone can become a leader—anyone who has the will and the courage to step forward, accept change and begin helping others transform themselves. These are the fundamental requirements of effective leadership.

Effective leadership isn't about playing God. Instead, it focuses on the God-given potential inherent in every man, woman, and child.

> **"The problems we face today cannot be solved by the same level of thinking that created them."**
> —*Albert Einstein*

Proven leadership finds the potential hidden within a person and brings it forth. The challenge of modern leadership is to find that potential and make constructive use of it. To that cause, anyone can aspire, and everyone should try.

Leadership is everyone's business

Those who believe leadership is for business or politics are simply contributing to the problem by refusing to acknowledge that they must at least lead themselves. If we don't lead ourselves, we will always be subject to the winds of societal change, finding ourselves more poorly prepared to confront each new assault.

We must prepare ourselves, then prepare our team members. Part of the process of preparing team members to cope with change involves changing organizational dynamics to better meet the challenges of internal growth and external competition. Organizational upheaval isn't necessary, but an attitude or paradigm shift is. Without such a shift, leaders won't be able to empower their team members.

This shift is also called "inverting the pyramid." In typical business environments, the organization can be thought of as a pyramid, with customer-service interaction at the bottom, followed by production, distribution, management, and finally, upper-level executives at the top.

What happens when we invert the pyramid? Simply stated, we put people where they belong—at the top of the pyramid. The leaders, now at the bottom of the pyramid, become servants. They convey their knowledge and expertise *up* the organization rather than letting it trickle *down*. Once turned upside down, each element of the inverted pyramid is free to lead itself. Rather than having the CEO provide leadership from the top of the pyramid, the organization provides leadership from all levels.

> **"Winning companies win because they have good leaders who nurture the development of other leaders at all levels of the organization."**
> —*Noel Tichy*

Everyone is a leader

The inverted pyramid is symbolic of a deeper truth that everyone leads, at least at certain times. The father, for example, may be a mail clerk at the office, but goes home at night to lead his family. The office secretary may sit behind a desk all day, but in the late afternoons she is coaching her son's Little League team. The buyer or sales rep may lead at church or in a community club. And quite often, a manager some distance removed from the executive suite may be the *de facto* leader of an entire organization.

We all lead at some point in our lives. The problem lies in how well we do the job of leading. In environments that we understand and control, we typically demonstrate solid leadership skills. Confronted with change and challenge, however, our veneer of leadership often cracks and crumbles. *If it is true that everyone leads, then it is also true that all of us could do a better job.*

That is what this book is all about. In these pages, we will discuss the application of leadership improvements. Ours is not a high-minded theoretical business treatise; instead, we offer a workable plan for making the most of your own leadership potential. Regardless of what you do or where you lead, you stand to improve your own results and those you achieve through other people. We believe our time-tested framework will help you and your team succeed.

What is leadership?

Part of the universal challenge of leadership is defining it in a way that will apply to virtually everyone. For example, one definition of leadership may be appropriate for a corporate CEO, but inappropriate for a weekend softball coach. Another definition of leadership may fit a professional golfer, but it misses the mark entirely when applied to the head of a civic organization. We apply differing definitions of leadership to elected officials, to family and societal leaders, and to religious figures. At some point, a single definition of leadership must be applied to all leaders, no matter who or what they lead.

At its core, leadership is *achieving specific, beneficial results through people.* This means that when we lead others as well as ourselves, we are charged with increasing *their* contribution in addition to our own. This is what all leaders do. The challenge is to increase results in a more consistent, efficient, and effective way.

To contribute more to the overall effort, regardless of what that effort might be, the leader

> **"I don't know what leadership is. But I know when I see it."**
> **—Dwight D. Eisenhower**

requires certain values...integrity, a servant's heart, and stewardship. To enable team members to contribute more to the organization, they must trust the leader and themselves, possess a commitment to the cause, and remain loyal and faithful to the effort.

Leadership may be many things, but there are also many things leadership is not. It is not a title, a position, a particular style, a particular set of personality traits, or a particular set of skills. These are merely the external trappings of leadership, not the true essence of leadership. None of these things by themselves define leadership, partly because leadership is a highly personal enterprise.

What is the leadership gap?

The leadership gap is more than just a literary analogy; it actually exists. As a leader or manager, you may see evidence of the gap in many ways:

- in the growing rift between leaders and team members
- in the increased dissatisfaction many team members and leaders feel in both their personal and work lives
- in your own search for a deeper meaning and purpose as you struggle to meet the daily challenges of moving your organization ahead.

Just as the leadership gap truly exists, so too the bridge that spans it. Every leader at every level has the potential to construct a bridge of personal and professional growth that will span the leadership gap. But until now, leaders attempting to construct such a bridge have typically met with frustration and disappointment; there were no blueprints to follow or signposts to guide.

This book is designed to fill that need.

The bridge that spans the leadership gap is made up of five pillars. Each pillar supports a vital part of the span that bridges the gap between leaders and team members. Like any blueprint, the five steps are easily understood and easily followed.

However, the strength of your leadership bridge relies on your own willingness to grow, to improve, and to change. Without that willingness, you will succeed in building only a shaky bridge that cannot stand the test of time. With that willingness, you can build a lasting bridge that will span the gap between you and your team members.

Progress, growth...and change?

Is change necessary? Are not some organizations essentially sound in structure, attitude, and spirit? Are not some businesses doing well enough as they are? Certainly, but the problem is that the environment in which these organizations operate is constantly changing. Leaders, team members, and their organizations must change to meet it...or face being swept away by leaders, followers, and institutions

20

who answer the call of change and grow to meet the demands of the times.

The bridge across the leadership gap carries with it an implicit message to leaders who are afraid to change: find someone who is unafraid and let that individual lead the team. In the final analysis, a frightened leader is a paralyzed leader. Such individuals allow inaction to suffice where action is demanded because they never really see the need for pro-active change. Highly effective leaders react to the changing times and conditions in a pro-active way. The end result is that they and their organizations are always one step ahead.

Today, those organizations that are a step behind will be left to wither away. Whether the end is sharp and quick or whether it is a slow, lingering demise, the outcome is still the same. Like it or not, every leader is faced with the awesome responsibility and mandate of change.

Change brings opportunity

The acceptance of change virtually guarantees a vibrant and thriving future, and that is where this book begin and ends. As a leader, you are the only one who can bravely and boldly grab hold of change and wring success out of it. If you do so, you'll find that the process of bridging the leadership gap offers astounding rewards.

For you, and for every member of your organization, the leadership bridge is the pathway

> **"Whatever you vividly imagine, ardently desire, sincerely believe, and enthusiastically act upon...must inevitably come to pass!"**
> —*Paul J. Meyer*

to dreams fulfilled, but you must first be willing to embark on this journey toward change. If you are willing, you can have it all!

But if you lack the desire or if your own spirit is weak, flawed, or faulty, you will find that the leadership bridge is always just beyond your reach. The opportunity to bridge the leadership gap knocks only once—it is knocking now. The decision belongs to you: will you answer that call? The choice is yours.

If you turn away, you may come to find your leadership experience hollow, unsatisfying, and empty of deeper meaning. Like change, the opportunity to bridge the gap is fleeting. If you do not choose to accept this challenge now, it may never return. But if you choose to build the bridge, you will reach each new level you desire.

Crossing the leadership bridge is a journey in and of itself, as much of a journey as your own life and career have been, and probably more of a trip than you and your followers are bargaining for! Your destination—the inevitable result of bridging the leadership gap by building upon the 5 pillars of leadership—is the fulfillment of your own leadership destiny. Your dreams are your inheritance; your vision is your birthright. Now is the time to begin to claim them for yourself and your colleagues.

A great confusion

It is no small wonder that leadership is so difficult to find these days, much less define. We hear so many conflicting voices and see so many examples that we aren't sure what to do:

- An office memo, for instance, might nag us to alter a particular procedure. We comply, unaware that we have just reinforced the notion that leadership is autocratic, top-down management concerned only with perpetuating the status quo.
- Madison Avenue hype tries to convince us to equate leadership with power and trappings.
- The inaction of bureaucrats often compels us to believe that leadership is a bottleneck that stops progress and stifles creativity.
- Leadership gurus try to convince us that by developing a few selected skills, we can instantly become qualified leaders on any stage.

All these messages—whether accidental or calculated—contribute to the overall confusion about the true nature of effective leadership. When all is said and done, leadership is simply how you achieve specific results through your own efforts and the efforts of other people. How you do it is your level of leadership.

Skills alone cannot produce effective leaders. Countless leaders through the centuries have discovered that mere skill is no substitute for key leadership values. Without a solid foundation of attitudes and productive habits, leaders will always fail to bridge the gap between themselves and their followers.

If skills alone were enough to produce a qualified leader, our society would not be crying out for more effective leadership! Skilled leaders are the equivalent of Calvin Coolidge's educated derelicts; they are literally a dime a dozen.

> **"If there is no transformation inside each of us, all the structural change in the world will have no impact on our institutions."**
> *—Peter Block*

Nor are leaders produced because they have developed personality traits like charisma and personal charm. What counts in today's world is the ability to translate skill and personality characteristics into results. The key to that process lies in values, attitudes, and the basic elements of achievement.

Five elements of achievement

The elements of achievement—also the five pillars of leadership—are easy enough to understand and practice. The problem is that they are not universally taught to leaders, and most often, they are ignored altogether. Any leader familiar with the process we've developed over the past four decades will recognize these elements immediately:

Element #1—define the specific results you wish to achieve.

Element #2—create a plan that, when followed, will achieve those results.

Element #3—develop the internal motivation necessary to take action.

Element #4—build the belief and confidence of yourself and your team members so that everyone performs at optimum level.

Element #5—instill determination so the team does not quit when confronted by problems or obstacles.

These five elements are the essential pillars of the bridge that will cross the gap between the promise of leadership and actual performance. No leader can be truly great without consistently practicing the habits represented by all five pillars. Contained within each pillar are attitudes that require more than just leadership skill to acquire and apply. All are essential to achieving specific results through leadership efforts.

Is the pathway to success really this easy to follow? Yes…and no. The elements themselves may be easy enough to grasp, but applying them requires diligent effort and patience. This is possibility thinking at its most direct and conscious level. The doubts that assail all of us—lack, limitation, and uncertainty—have no place here. Effective leaders remain focused on these five key elements as their power of concentration leaves them little time for fear, doubt, or worry.

Empowering leaders

For more than forty years, our companies have been empowering leaders to produce specific results and to overcome obstacles. We have worked with more than a million leaders in sixty different countries, helping them overcome the attitudes and habits that stand between themselves and leadership success.

Over decades of experience, we have pinpointed, identified, distilled, and focused on the key elements of effective leadership. Working with leaders from different cultures, different countries, languages, styles, and personalities, we have applied our development expertise with one clear goal in mind: To help these individuals become better, more effective leaders.

Hundreds of thousands of successful clients attest to the value of our process. ***What we do really works!***

Along the way, we felt it critical to identify the habits and attitudes that, combined together, can bridge the gap between the promise of leadership and actual leadership performance. What we present in this book is not hype or untried theory. This book contains the distilled essence of leadership empowerment, gleaned from working with over a million leaders worldwide.

Whether you realize it or not, the entire world is crying out for qualified, effective leadership. You were born with the potential to offer that essential quality to yourself and to others. As you work to bridge the leadership gap, you become

> ### 5 reasons why people fail to achieve
>
> **1st** - they lack determination, and quit before success is achieved.
>
> **2nd** - they lack a sincere belief that they can achieve the desired results.
>
> **3rd** - they are not motivated to take action.
>
> **4th** - they lack a plan—they have no real understanding of how they intend to succeed.
>
> **5th** - they do not know what results they are trying to achieve.

empowered to provide the answers that society is seeking. In giving of yourself and your experience, you empower yourself and your followers to conquer life's challenges and to share in more of life's abundance.

Leaders at every level know that while much has been given to them, much is also required. Building the five pillars toward highly effective leadership is a challenge, but effective leaders see this challenge as more of an opportunity. They know this is a chance to help themselves and their team members become more than they have ever been before.

Chapter Two

The 3 Foundational Elements to Leadership

Leaders should lead with one purpose in mind: to achieve increasingly positive results from the efforts of their team members. Highly effective leaders see qualities such as trust, commitment, and loyalty as absolutely essential for improving results from their organization. Imagine the power of an organization where every team member has complete trust, total commitment, and strong loyalty!

Many leaders, unfortunately, see trust, commitment, and loyalty as *byproducts* of success rather than the *causes* of success that they really are. This is a common misconception. The truth is that these qualities are developed in team members as a response to certain values already held by their leader, not as a result of increased productivity.

Values precede productivity

Highly effective leaders base their leadership on a foundation of three core values: integrity, a servant's heart, and stewardship. These are critical for growth in any organization and are what cause good, productive teams.

Leaders who want trust, commitment, and loyalty from team members must first develop these qualities themselves. They understand that integrity creates the effect of trust, a servant's heart generates commitment to the leader and the organization, and stewardship insures that team members develop to their full potential, which fosters loyalty. They also understand that no leader can convince team members to become something the leader is not.

The empowerment of individual team members can only happen when leaders display integrity, a servant's heart, and stewardship. Without these core values as the foundation, it will be impossible to lead effectively and bridge the leadership gap. A value-driven organization will not only bridge the gap, but it will be a leader in today's global economy where greater quality at lower cost is most important.

Such an organization will do more than survive—it will thrive! But outsiders always observe value-driven organizations, trying to uncover their competitive advantage. They are, however, looking in the wrong places. It is not the obvious, visible elements like production lines, manufacturing processes, or even highly talented individuals who create the identity of the effective organization. It is the intangible values that make the difference.

What too many observers do not realize is that without integrity, a servant's heart, and stewardship, it is impossible to build a truly effective team...or to become a truly effective leader.

These 3 core values are the 3 Foundational Elements to Effective Leadership:

Foundational element #1—Integrity

All great leaders display personal integrity by being dedicated to the pursuit of significant goals in all areas of life—not just goals for the organization. They lead well-balanced and well-rounded lives and offer their followers an opportunity to do as they do, not just as they say. This is integrity at its core.

Leaders are required to be individuals worthy of loyalty and genuine respect among those they lead. Leaders at every level cannot expect followers to do better unless leaders themselves are willing to improve.

Integrity is relatively simple to manage. It requires:

A. personal purpose and direction

and

B. balanced goals in all six areas of life

28

While the ***process*** of integrity involves personal analysis, the ***practice*** of integrity is an exercise in discipline. Integrity implies congruency. Congruent individuals display consistent thoughts and actions—their words and deeds do not contradict each other. Integrity generates a certain consistency in what people say, think, and do.

Some years ago, a consulting firm asked several top executives to cite the primary factor in their success. Integrity was consistently given as one of the top five reasons for business and personal success. Integrity begins at the personal level and naturally flows to the corporate level.

When leaders are motivated by their personal integrity, they:

- are better able to help team members perceive possibilities, develop pathways to success, and follow through to ultimate achievement
- ensure that working conditions are structured to develop and maintain positive, productive attitudes and habits for team members
- readily accept the responsibility for motivating others to use more of their full potential for success
- accept and internalize the responsibility for motivating themselves
- understand that it is their responsibility to help others strive to bring out the best in themselves.

Measuring your integrity

As a leader and role model, your integrity is measured by two compelling standards: an understanding of the long-term consequences, and whether your endeavor creates benefit or not.

The question of benefit goes deeper than concerns for profit or

> **"Character is the key to leadership. Research at Harvard University indicates that 85% of a leader's performance depends on personal character."**
> —*Warren Bennis*

opportunity; everyone connected to the endeavor must benefit and no one should be forced to lose. Long-term consequences should be carefully studied to the best of your ability.

In the final analysis, personal and professional integrity is easily measured by the leader's passion for achievement and by the leader's definition of success.

Foundational element #2—A servant's heart

Successful people in all walks of life share a common goal: to serve others. Leaders who lack the heart of a servant may enjoy temporary success, but they soon become disillusioned. They lose their concept of what their work is all about and lack credibility among team members and customers because they do not believe in what they are doing.

Highly effective leaders, on the other hand, succeed precisely because they are eager to serve others. They need no substitute value or ideal to gain success; instead, their servant's heart is an attitude and an essential value that helps to form a rock-solid foundation for effective leadership, and for lasting success and continuing achievement.

Hardheaded, hard-nosed managers and leaders may believe values-based leadership to be a weak alternative to heavy-handed management strategies; still others may believe that only weak leaders take the time to focus on potential, values, contribution and contentment.

On the other hand, leaders who possess a servant's heart:
- believe that team members have an intrinsic value beyond their tangible contributions to the success of the organization
- recognize the value of team members and the work they do
- desire to help and support every team member
- do whatever they can to support and facilitate the work of team members
- are themselves deeply committed to the growth of every team member

At the organizational level, having a servant's heart will enable leaders to coach, empower, and persuade those who follow. Without a servant's heart, such efforts will be mistrusted and less than effective.

With the global business climate shifting away from production of goods and toward a service orientation, leaders who respond to challenges with the heart of a servant actually empower their organizations to grow and prosper.

Leaders can have a clear vision, a strong mission, great goals, and elaborate plans, but if team members fail to put them into daily practice, the organization will ultimately fail. What team members actually do is what determines the success of an organization.

Leaders are finding that having a servant's heart produces unusual benefits:

- they are continually excited by what they do
- they are always full of enthusiasm about the results their customers and team members achieve
- they look forward to each new day with great anticipation
- they are always striving to build an active organization
- they are always surrounded by positive, productive team members

Leaders who possess a servant's heart are givers rather than takers; they are value-driven, but performance-oriented. Their mission is to lead team members to things the right way—and to do the right thing as well. They have their position in the organization precisely because they can live without it; highly effective leaders never try to hold on to an office or a title.

In contrast, leaders who try to succeed without developing a servant's heart must find a way to substitute for this key value. Whatever strategy a leader adopts, efforts to succeed without developing a servant's heart work only for a short while. Then, the leader is forced to try another method...and another, and another. Eventually, the individual ends up morally and financially bankrupt, and the people who should have been served drift away to find other suppliers and other employers.

Service—not a new concept

The concept of a servant's heart has been recognized by generation after generation of great thinkers and business people; it has even prompted some of the best-known business maxims of our time:

"The customer is always right!"

"The customer is king!"

"Our clients are our most valuable asset."

The Bible tells us that leaders must first be servants. By striving to develop a servant's heart, effective leaders are paying homage to this ancient success truth. And they are also making the most important investment of their life—an investment that has the potential to pay huge dividends if it is carefully nurtured and grown.

J. C. Penney, who built one of the world's greatest retail store chains, recognized the necessity of a servant's heart when he said that "life's greatest pleasure and satisfaction is found in giving, and the greatest gift of all is that of one's self." Former President George Bush put it best when he said, "Any definition of success must include service to others."

When top leaders demonstrate that they genuinely care about others, their team members respond to that attitude. The end result: team members want to contribute to the team and customers continue to buy. Surveys show that nearly two-thirds of all clients who stop doing business with one organization and start patronizing another, do so because of indifference. Indifference toward others is counteracted swiftly and surely by the development of a servant's heart.

When highly effective leaders invest in their organization by developing the desire to serve their team members and customers, the inevitable dividend is even greater success. When leaders possess a servant's heart, customers and team members know that they are appreciated and cared for because of the leader's follow-up and appropriate personal attention. Business and team members just naturally go where they feel welcome...and they stay where they are appreciated!

Having developed a servant's heart, successful leaders tend to:

- genuinely care about other people
- have a strong desire to serve

- believe in what they are doing
- like what they are doing
- pay attention to details, both small and large
- continually learn
- possess character, integrity and honesty
- make working with them a pleasure
- treat each customer and team member as someone special
- do more than they are paid for doing
- celebrate their team members' innate potential for success

Foundational element #3—Stewardship

Leaders who are servants develop a sense of responsibility—stewardship—over certain resources and assets. Stewardship becomes evident at a number of levels, depending on the maturity of the leader. The leader who is also a steward places emphasis not just on the bottom line, but also on the invaluable, intangible assets of an organization. The collective talent of the team is recognized as the core or human essence of the company or organization. True stewardship acknowledges human potential as the organization's most important asset, which means people are first.

Leaders cannot become truly effective and are never really committed until they are able to put the welfare of their team members ahead of themselves, their profit, and their own personal interests. Financial well-being is important to any business leader, but the quality that makes a leader truly great is seen in times of extreme financial stress. In a crunch, great leaders will cover their obligations to their employees and suppliers before they reward themselves. This is true stewardship.

In organizations that fail, effective stewardship has been the Achilles' heel of management. Some leaders are simply unable to subordinate their own needs and desires to those of the members of their team. Short-term pressures easily crowd out the long-term concern for developing people and their talents. The inevitable result: team members feel unappreciated and unwanted and fail to deliver their maximum contribution to the organization.

Highly effective leaders invest time, money, and attention in the development, nurturing, and protection of their team members' immediate stability as well as their long-term potential for success. They recognize the importance of serving as efficient stewards on behalf of the organization and its members. They recognize this as the key to the longevity and profitability of the organization, and on an even larger scale, the organization's impact on the economy and society through its continued offering of worthwhile products and services.

Is stewardship a fad?

Is stewardship another business management fad, like downsizing and outsourcing? Despite the publicity, fad-based management techniques fail to deliver the promised results. "Total Quality Management" programs have typically produced little improvement and organizational "flattening" tears apart complex internal communications and accountability structures. Downsizing can be similarly destructive.

During the 1990's, less than half of the firms that downsized saw long-term improvements in quality, productivity, or profitability. And outsourcing was the management rage until managers discovered it created more problems than it solved! More than a few companies found outsourcing so incredibly difficult to manage that outside production was brought back in-house.

Such management "solutions" often result in less loyalty from team members than before. The reason is obvious: the leaders' decisions and actions destroyed the very loyalty they were trying to establish.

Successful leaders believe stewardship is a vital, permanent part of their management effort. This is because they continue to see their team members as repositories of human potential. As stewards of potential, highly effective leaders feel an ongoing responsibility to help followers grow and develop in all aspects of their existence. If stewardship is a fad, the best leaders among us intend to make it a permanent one!

Every venture is an exercise in stewardship, a unique and synergistic partnership between the visionaries and those who work with them. Truly effective leaders create a partnership with their team members that goes far beyond the process of helping followers develop and improve themselves. Great leaders are able to mold a partnership that

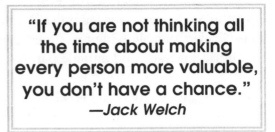

"If you are not thinking all the time about making every person more valuable, you don't have a chance."
—*Jack Welch*

enables leaders and followers to dream great dreams, make noble plans, and daily pursue those plans together.

If you fail to adequately develop the innate potential of your team members, you lose an incredible synergy (a combined energy that is invaluable and irreplaceable). If you lose it or fail to marshal it effectively, you and your team will function at a level far below everyone's capability.

Stewardship of human potential is an ingrained and ongoing part of the job of every effective leader. Two critical elements, 1) a keen sense of personal responsibility and 2) informal, on-site communication between leader and team members, help effective leaders and followers become balanced, content and productive. Instead of being a troublesome liability, team members contribute their potential to tip the scales of any business toward success and profitability.

The 3 partnership levels of stewards

The best leaders become stewards of potential by forming partnerships with their team members at three distinct levels:

First is the attitude level in which the leader can effect a positive impact on the team member's habits of thought. Most popular leadership "fads" and styles miss this level completely, focusing instead on goal-directed activity partnerships or skill-building partnerships. This omission is a huge mistake. Unless team members' attitudes remain consistently positive and productive, efforts toward reaching goals and building skills will create little impact.

Effective leaders form attitude partnerships by demonstrating empathy and concern for team members. This is a new experience for some leaders, but showing team members real care and concern is the first critical step toward attitude partnership.

Second is the belief level where effective leaders merge curiosity, knowledge, and interest. True to their foundation, they hold a deep and abiding belief in every team member, belief in their ability to do their job well, and belief in their potential for even greater accomplishment.

It is impossible for leaders to truly believe in something for which they care very little about. On the other hand, it's quite difficult for leaders to lack belief in their team members when they are interested in their team members' lives. When this is the case, leaders can easily see the true capability and potential of each team member, which further increases their belief in their team.

Third is the mutual acceptance level where team members are accepted as they are—with their human faults and failings. This is essential to marshaling their potential and helping them achieve. Effective leaders demonstrate acceptance by involving team members in the accomplishment of the organization's objectives.

At each of these levels, team members will not be too willing to accept—much less emulate—someone who requires them to change first. Effective leaders understand they must be the first to change before they can expect others to change. Unfortunately, many leaders and managers continue to focus only on developing the skills of their team members—to the exclusion of attitude, belief, and acceptance. They fail to understand that skill-building is truly effective only when the other partnership elements are firmly in place.

When leaders focus on skills in addition to the team members' own potential in all areas of life, the result is precisely what the leaders want: increased trust, commitment, and loyalty.

Values as a critical foundation

By developing the values of integrity, a servant's heart, and stewardship, leaders will achieve more of their own goals than they would by putting their personal concerns and needs ahead of values and principles. In fact, leaders who:

- desire fame…find it by helping to promote and develop others
- want to earn money…find it when they sincerely serve others
- want friends. .find them when they have the integrity necessary to be a friend to others
- want love…find it by loving others
- desire a sense of achievement…are stewards of human potential, dedicated to helping others succeed

When highly effective leaders possess personal and professional integrity, their efforts bring about solid and stable organizations that prosper, grow, and stand the test of time. When extraordinary leaders develop a servant's heart, they find a unique synergy that springs from their sincerity. The more they give, the more they have to give. The more they serve, the more they are able to serve.

And when aspiring leaders strive to become stewards of human potential, they begin to achieve their own personal goals while making a unique contribution to the lives of their team members.

Beginning today, what strategies can you devise to demonstrate to team members that you possess integrity? What steps can you take to begin to improve the corporate culture within your organization? And how can you help effect change in systems and processes, change that will help your team develop trust, loyalty, and commitment?

These are critical questions. In the end, you are the only one who can decide whether to adopt the attitudes and values conducive to highly effective leadership or whether to try to become successful without that critical foundation.

Take time to build a foundation that will stand the test of your success because a foundation of values that will stand the test of time.

Chapter Three

Building a Bridge on the
5 Pillars of Leadership

Some decades ago, a fifteen-year-old boy named John Goddard made a list of all the things he wanted to do in his lifetime. When he had finished the list, he had 127 items that became the blueprint for his life. Some of his earlier accomplishments were relatively easy: become an Eagle Scout, learn to type fifty words a minute, and study Jujitsu.

Some other goals Goddard set were a little more unusual: milk a rattlesnake, read the entire encyclopedia, and make a parachute jump. Then there were goals that to the average person might seem utterly impossible: climb Mt. Everest, visit every country in the world, and go to the moon.

Now the amazing part of the story: by the age of forty-seven, John Goddard had accomplished 103 items on his original list of 127. Goddard was motivated to identify important dreams and to begin working on them by hearing older people say, "If only I had done this or that when I was younger." He realized that too many people miss all the fun, excitement and thrills of life because they do not plan ahead. Making the list—creating the vision—was the beginning of Goddard's success.

Creating your bridge requires vision

Your efforts to create a bridge across the leadership gap should begin with the same sort of mission that motivated John Goddard to succeed. Certainly, that vision is not the same for every leader. For some, it may be achievement of a high political office, the accumulation of wealth, the creation of a large business organization, or the provision of a needed service.

While success does mean different things to different leaders, we've developed a definition that fits any vision for effective leadership: success is the progressive realization of worthwhile, predetermined personal and organizational goals.

Great leadership is not something that is created by accident; you can't buy it, inherit it, or create it with no effort or forethought.

> **Success is the progressive realization of worthwhile, predetermined personal and organizational goals.**

Instead, great leadership depends on following a lifelong process of goal setting and achievement. Highly effective leaders work to instill the mechanics of that process in the minds and hearts of their team members. Such a process operates through "progressive realization." Leadership success depends upon team and leader seeking predetermined goals.

This kind of success does not materialize through luck or by accident. Although many worthwhile achievements come as side effects of some other purpose, they are, nevertheless, a direct consequence of the pursuit of predetermined goals. We cannot always foresee the full ultimate effect of reaching a specific goal, but the important point to recognize is that achievement comes as a direct consequence of moving yourself and your organization toward predetermined goals.

An incident in the life of inventor Thomas A. Edison illustrates the relationship between predetermined goals and unanticipated accomplishments. While Edison was working on a complex problem related to telephone communication, he had an idea for producing a machine that would record and play back the human voice. He hastily

40

drew a sketch, handed it to one of his laboratory assistants, and said, "Build one of these."

That machine was the first phonograph, the forerunner of all the sophisticated recording devices we enjoy today. Edison's invention grew out of its relationship to a totally different problem he had set out to solve. Had he not been working toward a predetermined goal, this invention would not have been visualized.

Whether for yourself or for your organization, the goals you set must also be worthwhile. Many people today are spending their time much like Don Quixote, the windmill-tilter who chose to pursue numerous idealistic, impractical goals. Too many leaders lose any chance for effectiveness because they spend their time and

> **"If you are not now making the progress you'd like to make and are capable of making, it is simply because your goals are not clearly defined."**
> —*Paul J. Meyer*

effort chasing rainbows and making much ado about nothing. They are merely busy being busy; they never achieve anything worthwhile either for themselves or for their organization because their objectives are unworthy of their efforts. As a result, they themselves can never feel truly successful or highly effective.

Your goals must also be personally meaningful to you and those you lead and in line with your (and your team members') values, standards, and desires. Such goals will meet both personal and organizational needs.

When these requirements are met, you will find it possible to keep yourself and your team interested and committed to reaching specific goals. You will also find that your leadership bridge is taking shape before your eyes!

Putting your 5 pillars into place

To build a bridge that will span the leadership gap, there are 5 pillars of leadership that must be in place. When they are, and securely grounded in the proper foundation of integrity, stewardship, and a servant's heart, then you will be able to take yourself and your organization to heights that you have never dreamed of before.

The 5 pillars of leadership include:

Pillar #1: crystallizing your thinking

The first pillar in the support structure for your leadership bridge involves crystallizing your thinking so that you know where you stand now and where you want yourself and your organization to go. Remember, you and your team members will never reach goals by stumbling on them in the dark. You need a well-lit path and a well-conceived plan.

At this point, developing a mission, vision, and purpose for yourself and your team is critically important. Just as you and your family would not begin a vacation trip without a clear destination in mind, you must begin the journey toward highly effective leadership armed with a clear idea of where you are going and why.

The process of creating your own statements of vision, mission, and purpose actually help you to examine all six areas of your own life: financial and career, physical and health, family and home, mental and educational, spiritual and ethical, and social and cultural.

As you and your team members work to develop vision, mission, and purpose statements for your organization, those you lead will encounter the same need for the same sort of self-evaluation. Perhaps for the first time, your followers will develop a clear understanding of why they're doing what they're doing (the purpose behind their work). Additionally, the development of a team mission, vision and purpose helps members of your organization tie their personal success to the overall success of the business.

You and your team members may be able to generate an impressive list of organizational objectives. Quite likely, you will observe that some of the items on the list are in conflict with other items on the list. It becomes necessary then to assign a priority to each organizational goal or objective. Establish priorities according to a clear-cut system of organizational values—the truths you and your team hold dear and sacred. These values are revealed and created as your organization evaluates where it is and where it wants to go.

No one else can establish priorities for you and your team. The entire organization must accept the responsibility for setting priorities according to the team members' own unique sense of values and experiences.

Pillar #2: developing a written plan of action

The second pillar of the leadership bridge involves the development of a written plan for achieving your organization's goal along with deadlines for their attainment. It is extremely important that this plan is a written one, otherwise what seems crystal clear today may easily become vague or forgotten in the urgency of tomorrow's affairs. Written goals keep you and your team members on track, eliminating outside distractions and interruptions.

Additionally, written goals serve as a point of reference and a reminder of the organization's objective. A written plan for achieving your own personal goals also contributes to your effectiveness by conserving time and energy. Because you and your team know at all times where you want to go, it becomes easier to determine what to do next. A written plan also helps spot conflicts between various goals and values. As a team, you can then assign appropriate priorities before those conflicts produce personal frustration or sabotage your organization's goal-setting plan.

Setting a deadline for achieving your goal is extremely important. When you and your team members set a deadline, you act on the deadline because the deadline acts on all of you. A deadline alerts our body chemistry to react to the timetables you have set. As a consequence, you think, act, and react with urgency and with appropriate energy. Just as your muscles prepare in one way when you stoop over to pick up the morning paper and react in an entirely different manner when you prepare to lift a one-hundred-pound barbell, so your mind prepares your body and attitude for responding appropriately to the deadlines you have set for yourself and your organization.

Deadlines create a challenge, and you and your team members will find yourselves responding to that challenge. In competitive sports that include deadlines, the tension mounts as time runs out. The most exciting plays are often in the last few minutes, especially if the game is a close one, because people respond in dramatic fashion to the challenge of deadlines.

Deadlines also help you and your team members maintain a positive mental attitude. They focus attention and concentration on the key objectives at hand. They enable you and your team to eliminate distractions and to think clearly and creatively. You may have noticed that busy people are more positive than individuals who are idle. For you and your team members, physical and mental health are stimulated by the creative activity necessary to reach the deadlines you have set in the plans you've made.

Deadlines must, of course, be handled with mature understanding. You and not the deadline are the master. Sometimes through miscalculation or unforeseen circumstances, you and your organization will not reach a particular goal by the deadline you have set. Because you and your team set your own deadlines, you can change them. You can reset your sights in view of altered circumstances and change a deadline without abandoning the goal.

> **The mark of self-motivated individuals is their ability to distinguish between a setback and a defeat.**

In developing a written plan for achieving personal and organizational goals, defining the obstacles and roadblocks that might stand between you and your team and the achievement of the objective is of utmost importance. This part of the process is not merely making up excuses for something your organization has not already done. It is taking a realistic look at what you and your followers can expect as you work toward achieving a particular goal.

Pillar #3: creating desire and passion

The third pillar of support involves the development of a sincere desire among you and your team members to achieve personal and organizational goals. A burning passion for achievement marks the difference between a real goal and a mere wish. A wish or a daydream has no substance; it is vague, unformed, and unsupported by any action.

Desire, on the other hand, puts action into the plans you've made. Without desire strong enough to produce action, you and your team will achieve little, no matter how worthy the goal nor how workable the plan you've devised.

All of us are born with the desire to achieve, but we have also endured a great deal of conditioning. Some of us may have allowed our flow of creativity/desire to be cut off by outside circumstances and influences. When we rediscover the freshness, vitality and enthusiasm of the creativity/desire each of us possessed as a child, we are ready to achieve success.

Many people spend their lives dispensing effort in "minimum daily requirements," just like a prescription for vitamins. They rarely exceed the minimum effort required to get by. Actually, leaders and followers have vast reserves of strength like that experienced by athletes who run until exhausted and reach their "second wind." A sincere, burning desire for achievement triggers the willingness to capitalize on your full potential, and passion propels you and your team members toward the achievement of personal and organizational goals.

Successful leaders develop a genuine, driving passion for the achievement of personal and team goals. Without that passion, any leader is robbed of power, strength, and conviction. On the other hand, leaders who develop passion and channel their desire toward the achievement of individual and organizational objectives find their effectiveness and efficiency markedly increased.

Pillar #4: developing confidence and trust

The fourth pillar is your and your team members' ability to develop supreme confidence in yourselves and in your ability to achieve. For great leaders, nothing offers greater confidence than possessing clear-cut knowledge of planned actions and the order in which they should be taken. The mere existence of a written plan of action contributes immeasurably to your leadership effectiveness. The most important source of confidence you can have is knowing that you and your team can make the necessary internal and external changes that are needed for tangible goals to become a reality.

Many leaders experience difficulty in developing supreme confidence because they lack faith or confidence in the ability and performance of their team members. Highly effective leaders, on the other hand, understand that the process of achievement relies on altering basic attitudes and habits of thinking. When successful leaders learn to trust their team members to perform adequately, they have mastered a key factor in putting their organization's plan into action. When you have developed confidence and trust in the members of your team, you have laid the groundwork for firm and unshakable confidence in your organization's ability to succeed.

This kind of confidence in your team members is built on a firm foundation of personal rapport that grows rapidly as you share knowledge and experiences. But the development of such rapport implies that you must be personally involved with your team members. When you know from firsthand experience why a particular team member might be motivated to accomplish a particular task, you are incomparably more confident and trusting than you would be if you had merely assigned the task and walked away.

Leaders can always gain that kind of after-the-fact knowledge by assigning work and watching the results, but personal experience— the kind of individual interaction that turns superficial personal knowledge into practical confidence and trust—comes only from subjecting yourself and your team members to situ-

> **"It is fine to have ability, but the ability to discover ability in others is the true test."**
> —*Elbert Hubbard*

ations that require the exercise of your full potential. Once you recognize the significance of personal interaction and practical experience, you will find that you and your followers will actually welcome even the most stressful experiences. These stressful experiences are strong builders of confidence and trust.

Personal interaction with team members reinforces confidence and trust by providing a clear understanding of team member capability, of progress made, and of goals already achieved. As a result, highly effective leaders develop within themselves the attitudes of trust and confidence in their team members. Together with their followers, they begin to look for ways that things can be done instead of looking for reasons why they cannot be done.

Pillar #5: fostering commitment and responsibility

The fifth pillar supporting the leadership bridge is the development of a sincere commitment to follow through on your plan regardless of obstacles, criticism, or circumstances, and in spite of what others say, think, or do. This last leadership essential sets you apart from the mediocre multitudes of leaders and managers who yield to the pressure of society, the desire for acceptance, and the temptation to conform.

Ironclad commitment is not the same as stubbornness. It is, rather, the application of sustained effort, controlled attention, and concentrated energy. The development of commitment and the acceptance of personal responsibility for results are the hallmarks of your refusal to be dissuaded, sidetracked, or steered off course.

One of the techniques for developing this kind of commitment and determination is the use of the "act as if" principle. Begin to act as you will act when the goal is reached. Practice the leadership attitudes and habits you have chosen to develop. We learn to do by doing. Act out the leadership role you have chosen for yourself and believe in the possibility of reaching your goal. For you and your organization, the greatest motivator of all is belief.

The key to the development of ironclad commitment lies in the acceptance of personal responsibility for the success or failure of your organization, and for the achievement of your personal goals as well. All effective leaders realize that final success or failure rests largely in their hands. If success is to be transformed from a dream to a tangible reality, it is the responsibility of the leader to see the process through.

Asking yourself key questions

These five pillars mark the key points of the support structure for your leadership bridge. Some part of each pillar is already a vital part of your personality and some pillars are probably already better developed than others. As you work to strengthen and build upon each of these five pillars, you will notice that your effectiveness as a leader is increasing as well. You will also find that each of these pillars serves as a valuable template against which to measure every goal, every plan, and every activity.

Whatever you and your organization plan to do tomorrow, next week, or next year, ask yourself:

- Have I crystallized my thinking so that I know where I stand now and where I want to go? Are my vision, mission, and purpose clear to me and my team members?
- Do I have a detailed, written plan to achieve each important personal and organizational goal, and is there a deadline for its achievement? Are my personal goals balanced with the need to help my organization achieve? Do my personal goals represent a balance among the six areas of my life?
- Do I have a burning desire to achieve the goal I have set for myself? Have I developed within my team members and myself a passion for achieving the success we've envisioned?
- Do I have supreme confidence in our ability to reach our goal? Do I trust my team members to strive toward success and to continue to develop more of their innate potential for achievement?
- Have I accepted personal responsibility for the success of the team—and for the achievement of my own personal goals? Do I possess the iron-willed determination to follow through regardless of circumstances or what other people say, think, or do?

By applying the concepts and ideas outlined in the next five chapters, you can answer an unqualified "yes" to each of these questions. At that point, you will have built the five pillars necessary to bridge the leadership gap—and you will be ready to embark on a challenging new journey toward the exciting changes and achievements that lie on the other side.

Chapter Four

The First Pillar:
Crystallized Thinking

E ven in the rush of day-to-day activities, the most effective leaders take time to dream. They understand that a clear and unlimited vision—the ability to see themselves and their teams accomplishing great things—is their inheritance, their birthright, and their greatest single source of inspirational and motivational power.

But a grand vision can shrink to aimless wandering without careful thought and attention. Crystallized thinking moves dreams a step farther, honing and sharpening the aims and ambitions of unlimited vision into worthwhile goals and objectives. Successful leaders recognize that these goals, crystallized and well-defined, await only careful planning and the catalyst of actual effort. As the part of the leadership equation that spans dreaming and planning for achievement, crystallized thinking is one of the most valuable leadership commodities you can possess.

Top leaders crystallize their thinking to distill their unlimited vision. Crystallized thinking helps them identify the specific goals they want to achieve...and identify where they and their team stand now in relation to those objectives.

Almost every leader and manager experiences serious moments of soul searching. They ask themselves where they stand and where they want to go in various areas of life. Is this an exercise of unlimited vision and crystallized thinking? Usually not! These soul-searching interludes typically produce only vague, elusive answers...if they produce any answers at all.

First, know thyself

Clear-thinking leaders understand that developing a vision for their organization and crystallizing their thinking about goals and objectives requires first understanding themselves. The most effective leaders use crystallized thinking to determine exactly where they stand now and where they want to go. Only when leaders have examined themselves are they ready to examine and develop a course of action for their organization.

Socrates said, "Know thyself," but unfortunately his admonition failed to include specific instructions that would enable us to accomplish that feat! Because everyone's personality is complex, it is never easy for leaders and followers to know themselves. Specifically, motivation is subject to certain basic needs and drives that exert influence from within. And all of us are continually subject to many outside influences and pressures: conditioning from our family, our society, our environment, and our institutions. Still, conditioned habits of thought and action are fashioned by free choice, which is the same freedom that directs crystallized thinking and the objectives crystallized thinking will produce.

Knowing yourself and where you want to go also involves some degree of decision making. It also implies a certain amount of faith—there is never a point at which knowledge, information, or data is complete and totally accurate. Ultimately, you must act.

Second, crystallize your thinking

Highly effective leaders use crystallized thinking to arrive at a decision, and then they act on that decision. For them, crystallized thinking is the process that makes it possible to reach confident decisions about the goals they've chosen to pursue.Crystallized thinking is simply the act of clearly defining goals and objectives. *If you are dissatisfied with your present rate of progress compared to your true potential for success, your goals are not clearly defined.* Every achievement in leadership and in life is based upon that simple comparison. Every achievement in any area of life begins with the knowledge of current status and eventual destination.

Have you ever had a friend or relative call you from a nearby city and ask for directions to your home? If you are not familiar with that town, neither of you can determine an exact starting point for directions. Before the conversation goes anywhere, one of you has to crystallize your thinking about your current location so that you can find a common reference point for directions. The same holds true for your pursuit of success. You have to know exactly where you are before you can begin taking steps forward.

The same sort of crystallized thinking that brings highly effective leaders in touch with themselves and their potential is also the dynamic, shaping force that determines a course of action for the entire organization.

At that level, questions like these serve to define vision and focus thought on possibilities for achievement:

What do we want?

Asking this question helps isolate the specific dreams and desires common to both leaders and team members. What is the reason for your striving? What is the end result you seek? This is a fundamental question that you and your colleagues must answer before you can continue to narrow vision and focus.

Why do we want it?

This question seeks to uncover the true motivation behind your specific dreams and desires. Without this vital information, the quest for success at any level lacks real meaning. Additionally, this question may have several tiers. Suppose, for example, that you are motivated to develop a new production line because you want to have increased product to sell. You must first ask yourself: Why do you want increased product to sell? Do you desire the profit that will be made? Do you want a larger share of the market?

Why do we not already have it?

This question requires a certain amount of soul-searching. If a goal is important to you and your team, why is it not already a reality? Is it because you lack the skill? The capabilities? The motivation? What forces have kept you from achieving the goal before now?

Can we obtain it?

Leaders who try to provide definitive, concrete answers to the questions "Can we do it?" and "Will it work?" are deluding themselves and their team members. In any area of business or personal life, guarantees do not exist. But leaders *can* assess their present situation and the *likelihood* of future circumstances and events. This analysis points to a defining moment: leaders and team members must convince themselves

> **"If there is one thing that is clear from a century of leadership research it is this—leaders have a clear and often obsessive sense of what they want to achieve."**
> **—Paul Evans**

that the objective before them really *is* within their reach and grasp. Thus the question "Can we obtain it?" becomes a critical point that broaches either a commitment to action or reluctance to move forward.

How will we measure it?

This question demands some sort of accurate method of measuring success. Sometimes, the method may be a profit-and-loss statement. At other times, the method may incorporate intangible elements, like team member morale or community goodwill. A measuring stick should accompany every worthwhile endeavor. Finding these accurate methods of measurement requires crystallized thinking and a willingness to think "outside the box." Unfortunately, conventional thinking often restricts leaders and followers to methods that may no longer apply.

Whom will it affect?

Will those affected include only team members and leaders, or will they include customers, suppliers, and members of society at large? Many leaders make the critical mistake of underestimating the impact that follows their actions and decisions. Understandably, creating a small impact seldom motivates team members. The greater the impact, the greater the willingness to contribute to the overall effort.

Whom will it benefit?

Will the goal or objective benefit only the leaders? Will it benefit only those who work on the project? Will it benefit only team members? Or is there some greater benefit that extends outside the walls of the organization? Like impact, benefit is a powerful motivator. Many leaders shortcut its motivating potential by limiting their sphere of benefit. Goals and objectives should be selected based on criteria that center on benefit and impact. The larger and more widespread the benefit from achievement, the larger and more widespread the impact created.

Where will it lead us?

Answering this final question requires considerable leadership foresight and the ability to forecast trends and changes. You may find, as you consider tracking data and trends, that the goal or objective you've focused upon will not take you where you and your team members want to go. This is important information—information that enables you to alter your course before the goal takes you someplace you don't intend to go.

Crystallized thinking applies to the whole

All great leaders understand a simple truth: to get the organization right, they have to get the people right. But many leaders and managers just assume that once they themselves are "right," the organization will naturally follow a path toward stellar success.

This is a mistake for three important reasons:

First, owners, managers, and leaders may be "right" themselves—that is, they may see themselves as efficient and productive—but unless they have crystallized their thinking to develop a vision for the future of their organization, they cannot achieve success equal to their potential. The Scriptures tell us that "where there is no vision, the people perish." Where there is no vision, the business perishes as well.

When highly effective leaders have crystallized their thinking and know where they want the organization to go, they can then share those thoughts with the members of their team. Team members always want to know more—not less—about where the organization is going. The best leaders are always eager to provide that information.

Second, no organization can afford to remain static, repeating endlessly the behaviors that initially brought it success. Times change, people change, and business climates change. Highly effective leaders are prepared to welcome and embrace change instead of trying to run away from it. It may take years, even decades, but effective leaders understand that any organization that does not change is doomed to extinction.

Third, aspiring leaders cannot minimize the purpose for which the organization exists. The notion that a business exists solely to produce a profit is dangerously shortsighted. Each organization must also serve its own family of team members, its customers, and society in general.

But the expansion of a leader's thinking cannot stop there. All great leaders crystallize their thinking to help themselves and their teams know what they are striving to do, where the organization is going, and why leaders and team members are making the effort. Statements of mission, vision, and purpose are the hallmarks of crystallized thinking. They are the essential elements that must be in place before truly effective leadership can exist.

Developing a crystallized mission

For your organization, success always revolves around the progressive realization of worthwhile, predetermined goals. But before you move ahead to develop a plan of action to achieve organizational goals and objectives, first crystallize your thinking to determine your team's mission, vision, and purpose.

Whether for yourself or for your organization, a mission statement is a brief but powerful summary of your reason for existing. It provides direction, focus, and consistency for everything you and your team decide to do.

The sheer act of crystallizing your thinking can generate tremendous excitement and enthusiasm. But those effects are temporary. Once they wear off, a solid mission statement will help keep you and your team members on track toward the objectives you've set.

A mission statement is only effective, however, if team members know and understand it! In many companies, employees never really grasp the meaning of the mission statement. *In actuality, the livelihood of every member of the team depends on grasping both the words and meaning of the mission statement.* If rank-and-file employees fail to understand and internalize it, it is management's fault. Indeed, this lack of understanding and singleness of purpose can eventually contribute to any leader's downfall.

Just as you and your organization have mission statements, each member of your team should have one as well. Personal and business mission statements serve as a foundation for guiding decisions, actions, and goals in both career and private life.

The "sensational" business decisions you read about in the business section of your daily newspaper are usually made by companies operating without mission statements. Something spectacular may happen that receives a lot of attention, but over time, because there is no crystallized thinking or grand design guiding the actions of these managers and leaders, they will stray further and further away from their potential. These individuals have typically lost sight of their true purpose—both personally and in a business sense—because they haven't been able to crystallize their thinking and focus their collective creativity on special impacts and outcomes. Their oversight detracts from and may destroy the contribution, impact, and success of their organization.

Look at your own organization's mission statement. (This assumes, of course, that you have one in place. If not, crystallized thinking will help you create one quickly and efficiently.) Work to make the mission statement as succinct and brief as possible. Why? Because you cannot expect your team members to understand, accept, and internalize a mission statement that they cannot memorize.

A concise, well-written business mission statement is the epitome of crystallized thinking. It describes the purpose of the organization in terms relating not only to product or service marketed but also in terms of who comprises the market for the product or service, how the product or service benefits the consumer, and how the business will benefit from success. Most successful leaders know they will be unable to achieve their goals unless everyone involved in the process can achieve their own goals.

In the final analysis, the input of every team member will probably be necessary to construct a complete, concise, well-balanced mission statement. Admittedly, you'll need patience and a long-term perspective if you want to capture the thoughts and ideas of every member of the team, but the result is even greater dedication and involvement from every individual. Great leaders have discovered this fundamental truth: they cannot lead without listening.

By paying close attention to team member input, leaders can chart an organizational course that will closely parallel the dreams and desires of rank-and-file workers as well as leaders and managers. The definition this process gives to the organizational culture, as well as the pride it generates, elevates the organization's ability to attract and keep good team members. Team members who are excited to "be on board," dedicate themselves to the group's mission more readily than those who are unsure that they have made a wise career move. The inevitable result of everyone catching the same vision is a more closely-knit group of individuals who are unified to achieve a long-range common goal and who are committed to the same central purpose.

Putting forth the effort required to crystallize your thinking and to define the mission of yourself and your team will reward each of you with a solid, stable foundation for future achievement. Just as the strength and stability of your foundation determines the heights to which you and your organization can aspire, so your mission statement, coupled with your commitment to developing your team, will effectively predict the eventual success of the business.

Creating a crystallized vision

A mission statement tells your team members and customers what the business does, while a vision statement lets them know where the business is heading. If a mission statement is a critical element in developing highly effective leadership, then a vision statement should be regarded as something even more vital.

For you, crystallizing your vision makes the process of becoming an effective leader much easier. For your associates, a concise vision identifies your overall business goals and links their goals to yours.

Without a vision statement, many of your team members are likely to feel that they are a part of something quite ordinary—something drab, dull, and lacking direction. The vision statement sets the tone for the future of the company. It should be exciting but brief; it should convey a sense of urgency and a clear sense of corporate destiny.

If you want to be a highly effective leader, take a good look at your vision statement. (If you don't have one, you need to set about creating one today!) A vision statement defines the future; every day you work without it, you are working for yesterday rather than for tomorrow. Your vision statement should be a conduit or channel for your goals and expectations. It should challenge you and your team members to a bright new future without burdening anyone with the mistakes and poor choices that may have been made in the past.

While a mission statement is largely a consensus of crystallized thinking, a vision statement may not require input from every member of your team. If you own the business or help lead it, you are the individual who should determine—or at least help determine—what the future holds. Truly successful leaders know where the organization is headed. Their crusade focuses on leading team members along that predetermined pathway to success.

While your mission statement represents the reasons you and your organization continue to exist, a vision statement serves a higher purpose: it tells the world what you intend to do with the gifts and talents your Creator has given you and your team members.

Inspiring a crystallized purpose

A statement of purpose simply states why you and your team are making the effort to succeed. In the greater scheme of things, a statement of purpose should probably come before mission and vision statements. After all, the motivation for action must precede the action itself. Many businesses and highly effective leaders already have mission and vision statements, albeit overly wordy and imprecise.

So why save the statement of purpose for last? Largely because it requires the highest degree of deliberate, crystallized thinking, which is the prime reason why most leaders and organizations lack anything resembling a statement of purpose. A statement answers one fundamental question: "Why am I doing what I'm doing?"

This question applies as much to you personally as it does to the organization to which you belong. It also applies to every person who helps you in the effort to be successful.

So, why are you doing what you're doing?

This is a personal question; no one can answer it except you. You are also infinitely more qualified to decide your purpose than anyone else is. So, what is your overriding purpose? Is it money? Is it your family? Are you doing it all for your team members? For your community? For society in general? For God? Only you can decide.

Your statement of purpose should be as brief and to-the-point as are typical mission and vision statements. *All three statements combined should require less than a hundred words.* You've probably seen companies and organizations use more than 70 words just for their mission statement. Which do you expect would be more memorable?

Crystallized thinking and the future

Remember, if you are not now making the progress you would like to make and are capable of making, it is simply because your goals are not clearly defined. If you want to move forward to develop your organization's full potential for success and achievement, clear and concise mission, vision, and purpose statements are essential.

These statements can no longer be thought of as buzzwords or the latest business fad. They cannot be considered the exclusive property of commercial intellectuals and business consultants. These statements should have been a part of every business enterprise since the dawn of commerce. Had they been, we would all be much more successful today.

Why? Because written mission, vision, and purpose statements crystallize thinking—and crystallized thought motivates action. If you fail to crystallize your thinking or decide to ignore the creation of your unique mission, vision, and purpose statements, you choose to consign yourself and your organization to the dustbin of business his-

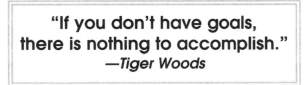

"If you don't have goals, there is nothing to accomplish."
—*Tiger Woods*

tory. Your organization and team may not collapse tomorrow, or next week, or even in the next decade. Sooner or later, though, the lack of crystallized thinking will drive you and your followers into the ground.

Take the time to think through what you do, why you do it, and where you want to go. A few moments of creative thinking pay huge leadership dividends. In quiet moments of solitude, leaders renew their strength. Seize this time to remind yourself of your personal and business mission, vision, and purpose.

Finding opportunities to crystallize your thinking may require pulling away from the alluring addiction of seemingly urgent tasks. You pause and refocus because you yearn for lasting achievement and significant meaningful success. Investing time and emotional energy into crystallized thinking refreshes your inspiration, motivation, and creative energy.

Crystallize your thinking today!

Chapter Five

The Second Pillar:
Plans & Balance

The next step toward maximum effectiveness involves the development of written plans for the achievement of specific objectives. These objectives are the goals that move the team forward and help both leader and team members develop personally. Just as a sprinter has a finish line to cross, so every individual, from leader to follower, has goals to attain.

Written plans help determine both how and when you and your team will cross the finish line. Will you run straight down the lane to your goal? Or will you move from side to side, experiencing the path to achievement in a different way? The decision is yours. Like the decisions you've made through crystallized thinking, you can't afford to abdicate your control over the process now.

For the sprinter entering the last lap, it is time to take longer strides. For you, it is time to write down your plans and goals. Written plans are essential if you intend to push your goal beyond the realm of daydreaming. With plans clearly detailed and carefully drawn, you cut through any confusion your own thought process may have created. Whether you consider your leadership journey a sprint or a marathon, written plans allow you to convert theory into practice, thought into action, and dreams into reality.

The importance of written plans

Developing written plans carries with it an impressive benefit: it minimizes the tendency to procrastinate. The plan itself creates an "inspirational discontent" with things as they are. Truly effective leaders clearly visualize the attainment of the goals they set. These objectives appear to them as accomplished fact, even before they start down the road to achievement. As a result, highly effective leaders are more committed to a particular plan of action and are more confident in their ability to achieve the goal. Energy, excitement, and enthusiasm are all stimulated by written plans of action. Rather than wondering when or if they should start, highly effective leaders can hardly wait to begin.

If you are unable to write something down, you cannot crystallize it. If you cannot crystallize a goal into a written plan, you will probably never make the goal a reality. Written plans for achieving goals are often works of art in and of themselves.

Typically, written plans contain these 5 essential elements:
1. the goal, written in a clear and concise manner
2. a deadline or target date for the achievement of the goal
3. a summary of benefits to be gained and losses to be avoided as a result of achieving the goal
4. a summary of possible obstacles to achievement, along with written strategies for overcoming these roadblocks
5. a step-by-step plan for the achievement process

Putting goals on paper serves as a commitment to achievement. Successful people rely on written plans as guideposts in the quest to develop each area of life. For one to become an extraordinarily successful leader, written plans are the second essential element.

The challenge of balance

Exemplary leaders use written and specific goals to develop a keen sense of balance in themselves and the members of their team. The pathway to this unique sense of balance is the road to becoming a Total Person.

To become a Total Person and a complete leader, first focus on achieving your full potential as an individual. Second, commit to growing personally by setting and striving toward achieving challenging goals in six key areas of life: Family, Financial, Mental, Physical, Social, and Spiritual. Each of these six areas demands excellence from all of us—and each area is a benchmark of the Total Person process.

Why is it imperative for a highly effective leader to first become a Total Person? Simply stated, leaders are role models. If they overlook one or more of the six areas of life, they automatically develop something of a lopsided existence. Regardless of status or station in life, an out-of-balance life makes for some rather painful progress up and down the hills of human experience. When leaders display a lopsided existence, the integrity of their leadership is compromised as well.

This "bumpy ride" is responsible for most of the difficulties that plague modern society. Individuals who are deficient in one or more areas of life tend to warp and distort the other areas. Warped lives are not just created by accident or circumstance. Instead, they are the result of deliberate choice, the inevitable consequence of the neglect and abandonment of various aspects of life. The result is an out-of-round individual, someone who is out of balance and often out of control as well.

Let's examine the six areas of life that make up the Total Person:

Family – Family goals affect you and those you love. They are usually goals that guide your interaction, define your commitment, and create a cohesive sense of worth that binds you to those you care about.

Financial – Financial goals affect earnings, savings, and investments. Financial goals govern how you earn, acquire, and use financial leverage. Financial goals also relate to career advancement, business contribution, and your personal legacy to those you love.

Mental – Mental goals focus on expanding the mind. Mental goals allow you to gather knowledge that leads to improvement of your spirit and condition. Mental goals direct your quest for mastery of any subject or skill. Mental goals guide you toward intellectual pursuits and help you experience the true joy of learning.

Physical – Physical goals help you improve your body. Physical goals govern the kind of physical shape you are in or wish to attain. Physical goals may also focus on recreation and sporting activities you enjoy. Physical goals deal with your overall health and fitness.

Social – Social goals strengthen your ability to interact personally with others. They help you engage in new and different experiences, meet new people, and accept new challenges to live and work with others.

Spiritual – Spiritual goals affect your relationship with your Creator. These goals bind you to whatever faith you profess. Spiritual goals create and tie you to certain ethical standards of moral behavior and conduct. Spiritual goals can help you express your own religious philosophy.

No one—regardless of lifestyle or status—can be considered a Total Person unless he or she has developed significant goals for each of these six areas of life. Likewise, no one can become a highly effective leader without becoming a Total Person first. And no one can attain Total Person status without a clear-cut purpose or overall reason for living.

The neglect of any one of the six areas leads to the abandonment of Total Person status. The essential element of lasting success, personally and in a leadership position, is balance.

The Wheel of Life

The six areas of life can be compared to the spokes of a wheel. Each spoke radiates out from the center of the wheel (the center of your life) to the rim. It's quite possible that, given a lack of focus on one or more areas, some spokes will be longer than others. In fact, some spokes may be quite short. Only a few spokes may actually be long enough to reach the rim.

As you might expect, spokes that don't reach the rim can create a Wheel of Life that is shaped more like a triangle or a trapezoid. A lopsided wheel will not roll very fast, if at all. This is precisely the effect that ignored areas of life have on the Total Person—they grind all forward progress to an eventual halt.

For you to become an effective leader, it is important that each spoke of your wheel—each of the six areas of life—be adequately developed. If, for example, you focus on four areas and neglect the other two, your forward progress will still be severely handicapped.

Only by developing a well-rounded wheel can you be assured of making the kind of progress necessary to reach your goals, lead others effectively, and utilize more of your God-given potential.

The result of neglect

Regardless of their level of effectiveness, leaders are often extraordinarily busy people. Indeed, you may feel that you are already running at peak potential and that you have no more time, no more energy, and no more effort to give to becoming more than you are. It is, however, a grave mistake to ignore various areas of your life simply because you believe you cannot spare the time or effort required to develop them.

Why? Because you have probably not yet reached your "second wind." This "second wind," as athletes know, only shows itself when the first wind has been completely exhausted.

Additionally, believing that you need not devote time and attention to a certain area of life consigns you to failure in one or more other areas. Because you believe you are already running at top speed on the road to success, it's a good bet that one or two areas are already suffering the effects of neglect. The end result will be a Wheel of Life that is severely out-of-round.

Most successful leaders have found that living life out-of-balance actually causes them to slow down because they are forced to divert their focus to problems that occur when they ignore other areas of life.

If we carefully observe individuals who contribute to the continued decline and destruction of modern society, we find that they typically lack an understanding of the need to become a Total Person. Because these individuals lack goals and objectives in the key areas of life, anything approaching a balanced existence is an unreachable ideal for them.

A basic human tragedy is that most of these individuals have a severely limited belief in themselves and their potential for success. They have never taken time to examine life as a whole; never bothered to think about different areas of life. As a consequence, they have never learned the art of straightening and strengthening the wheels of their own lives. Their neglect is our neglect. Many of us have been content enough to let these individuals go their own way, so long as their paths did not cross ours. Efficient and effective leaders look for ways to make paths and human potential intersect. These crossroads are an opportunity to teach, coach, and direct. They represent every leader's best chance to help others bring out the best in themselves.

Showing your team members how to develop their full potential and create a balanced existence creates a common bond between you and other committed leaders and between you and the members of your team. It is this process—the development of yourself and your people, and the development of individual wheels of life—that is the essential element of highly effective leadership.

Your personal assessment

Where do you stand now in each of the six areas of life? Think carefully about your status in each area of life. If "10" represented perfection and "1" only minimal impact, where would you rank yourself? Where would you mark your progress in each area of life?

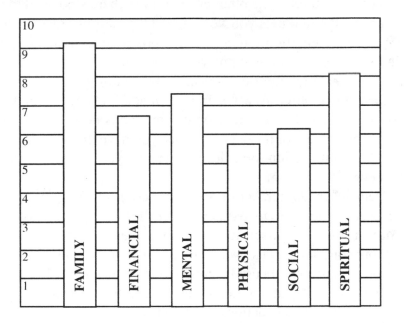

Take a few moments to think about your life as it is today. Then mark each area of life to reflect your honest evaluation of where you stand now in relation to your potential for success. Be as honest as possible; no one need see the chart but you. When you've finished marking the chart and are satisfied with the rankings you've assigned yourself in each area of life, transpose those numbers back to the Wheel of Life. Then clockwise connect the dots.

Is your Wheel of Life round? How well would it roll through life? Which areas of life need the most work? In which areas of life do you currently excel? In which area could you create the greatest immediate impact? Which area would take the most time to improve? What goals can you begin to achieve today that will contribute to a more rounded wheel?

Many leaders who have achieved extraordinary success in the business world are dismayed to see that their own self-evaluation indicates dramatic need for personal improvement. If this is true for you, you may find yourself feeling downcast, depressed, or even angry about where you stand in the other areas of life. There's no need to feel dejected about the rankings you've assigned the various areas. Instead, turn any negative emotion into a positive, productive passion—a genuine enthusiasm for making appropriate changes.

Begin making significant changes by setting goals and priorities in each area of life. You will find even small changes significant and exciting! Then, develop the step-by-step plans necessary to guarantee the achievement of those goals. Once you have the plans in place, it's time to get into action to achieve the results you want...and to cast a better-rounded Wheel of Life.

Remember, 90 percent of all failure comes from quitting. The reverse is also true: you are 90 percent of the way to your goals the moment you commit yourself to their achievement.

Your conscious focus is determined by your subconscious intention. If you are sincerely focused on improving your standing in a certain area of life, you find that you begin paying attention to that area. As a result, your subconscious actions allow others to see your immediate improvement as well. When those you lead see you change, your actions and behavior offer strong validity to your acceptance and internalization of the Total Person concept.

Goals for the Six Areas—*an overview*

Determining where you stand in each of the six areas of life may be a slightly painful process, but it is a necessary one if you are to give direction to your dreams. The process can also be an enjoyable one as you relive and recognize the success you've achieved so far in each area. And gaining self-knowledge through this kind of self-examination process can also be extremely stimulating; you develop a well-balanced awareness of who you really are now. This is valuable information as you explore the kind of individual you wish to become.

All of us are tempted to keep doing the things we do best. This is because we all possess unique strengths and abilities that we enjoy using. However, we also have certain shortcomings and deficiencies that we often wish to ignore. As a highly effective leader, you recognize not only those talents and abilities you put on display, but also the hidden weaknesses that you seldom think about or admit. Were you to continue to hide your deficiencies, they could well sabotage your efforts to become a balanced individual. Ultimately, they might affect your success and the success of those you lead.

When you are satisfied with the overview you've created, you're ready to move ahead to set concrete goals in each of the six areas of life. This process demands that you decide what comes first, second, third, and so on. Your own values will serve to guide you in selecting those items that will have greatest priority for you.

Once you've established priorities, you will probably be able to picture the end result of achieving the goals you have set. This is a critical test, for without a clear mental picture, the results you obtain will likely be blurred or distorted—much like taking a picture with an out-of-focus camera. *There is no way to achieve a clear-cut goal unless you begin with a clear-cut mental picture of the result the goal will produce.*

Criteria for goal direction

As a leader, you already know the benefits that are yours when you become goal-directed. But since setting goals is often a generic practice, you may not be aware that the goals you set in each area of life must meet five criteria if they are true goals. Odds are, your goals are wishes—vague and unformed to some degree.

First criteria: Goals must be written and specific. William James told us a century ago that writing crystallizes thought and crystallized thought motivates action. If you find yourself unable to set down a goal in writing and describe it in vivid detail, then your thinking about the goal has probably not crystallized to the point of sharpness and clear definition. Hazy goals produce, at best, hazy results. Typically, they produce no results at all!

Second criteria: The goals you set must be your own personal goals. Of course, no one else can set goals for you because no one else has your own particular view of what must be accomplished. Nor does anyone have your own unique personality, your abilities, your needs, or your potential for success. Seeking goals that have been set for you by others is tantamount to pursuing borrowed goals, and though they may be positive and productive in and of themselves, they can never generate the levels of passion, desire, and determination required for you or anyone else to achieve them.

However, when your team members achieve a goal they've set for themselves, they see it as a meaningful victory because the goal was personally meaningful.

Third criteria: Your goals must be stated positively. While you are able to form a clear mental picture of yourself taking some positive action, it is impossible to see yourself not doing something! Your goals must create a vivid mental image—an image of you taking action to achieve them!

You may have noticed that those you lead often set negative goals. "I will not waste time," one person says, while another maintains, "I will not be late." Their goals would work better if you helped them state the objective in positive form: "I will make productive use of my time" or "I will arrive at the job on time."

Fourth criteria: Goals must be realistic and attainable. This is not to say that goals you set in any area of life must be commonplace or ordinary. Indeed, a mediocre goal will hold little motivation for you; a high goal is usually easier to reach than a low goal. A realistic goal represents an objective toward which you are both willing and able to work.

The attainability of a goal, on the other hand, is a question best answered by the goal's unique timetable. Long-range goals often hold less motivation than short-range goals. The key to accomplishing long-range objectives, then, is to set intermediate steps that will keep you on track and give you confidence to continue on the journey. Short-range goals, on the other hand, serve to broaden your vision. Goals that were unimaginable only days ago now move into view, and your new vantage point allows you to see greater opportunities to express your innate potential.

Fifth criteria: The goals you set must include personality changes. This is not to say that every goal you write down must require you to change personally. Instead, you and your team members must take required personality changes into account as you plan for the achievement of specific objectives. You may find that your team members will frequently set goals *to have* without setting goals *to become*. Unfortunately, the process doesn't work this way.

All of us must set intangible goals of becoming—of developing the required personality characteristics—before we can legitimately set goals of a more tangible nature.

Steps to becoming a Total Person

The path toward becoming a Total Person begins with 3 very important steps:

#1) determining your most important objectives in each key area of life

#2) planning for the achievement of those objectives

#3) taking daily action on your plan

#1—Determining most important objectives: Each objective is an opportunity for personal and organizational improvement—an opportunity to set and reach challenging goals that will help ensure the proper and positive development of yourself and your team members.

This involves assessing and reviewing strengths and weaknesses in each area of life. Carefully examine your strengths and compare them with your opportunities to improve. Then take a moment to ask yourself another question: "What one thing would I like to see happen in this area of my life?"

Next, decide what comes second...and third...and fourth. Again, don't limit your imagination by taking into account the time, effort, or money required to make your vision a reality. Concentrate on making as long a list of goals as possible for each area of life.

Write down as many items as you can. You may be able to jot down only two or three ideas or you may find that your imagination offers up an inexhaustible supply! Again, strive for quantity of items at this point. When you believe you've developed a complete list, double-check to make sure some of the items you've written down offer strength or fulfillment for some of the weaknesses you've identified.

Once you're satisfied with the length of your list, give each item a reality check by working to transform it into a SMART goal—a goal that is Specific, Measurable, Attainable, Realistic, and Tangible. Strive to restate each idea you've written so that it meets the SMART goal criteria.

If an item cannot be restated as a SMART goal, there is an underlying reason. Is this item a mere wish or a daydream? Have you crystallized your thinking about the goal? Do you believe it's somehow unattainable?

You may find that the item will forever be a vague, undefined wish. Or you may need to combat some mind-induced roadblocks that keep you from seeing your daydream or wish as a goal to be achieved.

Repeat the process for each of the other five key areas of life. This may take some time, so take as long as you need and avoid the temptation to rush the job. When you've begun your list of goals for all six key areas of life, you must again make the power of choice work for you.

#2—Planning for achievement: For each key area of life, your list of goals and opportunities for improvement may be quite long or it may contain only a single item. Most likely, each of your lists will contain several important items. Whatever the length of your individual lists, you will need to prioritize the items—to decide what comes first, what comes second, and so on.

Items that were previously considered critically important may need to be put on the back burner to allow for the accomplishment of another critical item. Highly effective leaders follow the habit of prioritizing goals and objectives, which is why they always know what they wish to do next after an item is completed.

#3—Taking daily action: From the list of priority goals in the six areas of life, create a list of things you must do today to make progress toward the top item in each area. Successful leaders strive to take positive, determined action each day to ensure that they make progress toward the achievement of worthwhile goals and objectives.

The action steps you must take today may seem small or relatively inconsequential. This is not a cause for concern, as long as you move slightly forward each day, you will eventually develop each area of life.

What will your action steps be today? Perhaps you'll find time to begin reading an important article in a management magazine. Or you may wish to read from Scripture or visit your church or synagogue. You may want to discuss new concepts, ideas, and events with your team members and others around you. You might have your assistant call an equipment supplier and request brochures on new machinery. Additionally, you may want to spend a few minutes catching up your checkbook or spot-checking your investments.

Whatever your goals, the important thing is to begin now. Get up and take action! Highly effective leaders do something daily so that the goals and dreams they cherish blossom into reality.

Where do you want to go?

Your choice of goals for each of the six areas of life must be uniquely personal and based on your own value system. No one else can decide which personal goals you should pursue; you must choose them yourself. Avoid agonizing over the selection of your goals; organize your dreams and desires and construct your goals from those basic elements. If you squander time and potential wondering about making the "right" choice of a goal to pursue, you will find that your team members will squander their time and mental energy doing exactly the same thing.

Over the last three decades, our companies have seen tens of thousands of clients set some extraordinary goals. We've found it helpful to provide aspiring leaders with a thought-stimulating list of sample goals—not with the idea that any goal on the list would become a part of their personal goals, but rather to help our clients begin the thought process necessary to create meaningful objectives to pursue.

Here are a few examples:

In the financial area, your goals could include:
- Earning a promotion to vice-president of the company
- Buying a luxury family car
- Increasing your income by 10 percent
- Upgrading your personal computer

In the family area, your goals might include:
- Taking the family to Hawaii for a vacation
- Moving to a larger home
- Spending more time with your children

- Enjoying a weekend away with your spouse each quarter

In the physical area of life, goals could be:
- Learning CPR
- Developing a consistent first serve in tennis
- Weighing 175 pounds
- Working out three times per week

In the social area, objectives might be:
- Joining a community discussion group
- Joining a golf club
- Meeting the parents of your children's friends
- Having a dinner party in your home

In the mental area, goals could include:
- Reading a new book every week
- Taking an advanced computer course
- Subscribing to new magazines or trade journals
- Teaching a community business class

In the spiritual area, you might set these goals:
- Providing consistent spiritual leadership to your family
- Doubling your financial contribution to your place of worship
- Developing a code of ethics with your team members
- Reading a chapter of scripture each day

Certain goals can easily fit into two or three areas of life—they are not confined to just one. How do you know that a particular goal belongs in a particular area? You choose to put it there! Just as no one can tell you what goals to set, so no one can tell you whether a particular objective is a spiritual goal or a mental goal. That new car, for example, might be either a family goal or a financial goal, or it could be a social or mental goal. You choose where to place the goals you've set according to your own value system and your own definitions of each area of life.

The important thing, of course, is to set goals in each area—goals that will help you develop a sense of direction and fulfillment in every area of life. Don't agonize over the placement of the objectives you've set for yourself. Organize them and begin to work on the process of making them happen in your life.

Again, the items on our list of sample goals are just that—samples. They are not intended to replace your own unique personality, your own needs, and your creativity. To inspire and challenge you, goals must be personally meaningful to you—not borrowed from someone else. And as you share the Total Person concept with your team members, make sure that the goals they set are their own goals, not yours or someone else's.

Priorities for balanced leaders

Decades ago, traveling fairs and carnivals usually featured a plate spinner—someone who spun china plates atop sticks. Often plate spinners would spin five or six plates at a time, and they could keep them all spinning for hours. Of course, plate spinners learned the hard way not to pay too much attention to one plate; the others had a way of falling off and breaking if they were neglected.

So it is with your Wheel of Life. If you place too much emphasis on any one area, you risk breaking up your hard work and progress in the other areas. Being a Total Person is a bit like being a plate spinner—you must focus on all six areas at once.

> **"Golf is the easy part. The hard part is trying to balance your life."**
> —*Tiger Woods*

Of course, efficient and effective leaders can successfully pursue several goals at once, but they cannot try to achieve every goal they've set simultaneously. By managing yourself to accomplish, say, six to ten goals at a time, you can make sure that each area of life is well represented. You can also ensure that you do not devote too much time to any one goal or any one area of life.

78

Similarly, you'll want to share this balancing technique with your team members. Without it, they may lead more goal directed lives, but their Wheels of Life will remain out-of-balance and out-of-round.

Which goals will you choose to work on first? The question is most easily answered by examining your list of goals in each area of life. Select your first goals according to your own personal criteria: most important, easiest, fastest to accomplish, and so on. Only when you choose initial goals from your list and develop written plans to accomplish those objectives can you begin to take action—action that will contribute toward becoming a Total Person.

The leader as role model

As you embark on the journey to become a Total Person, you will find that you take a significant step toward bridging the leadership gap. This is because the Total Person process actually enhances the five pillars of effective leadership. Members of your team respond to you in a new and more meaningful way because they see and sense changes in you that make you more worthy of emulation and respect.

Specifically, the Total Person process produces a rapid improvement in your own self-image. As you make even minimal progress in the various areas of life, you may find that you are praising yourself, if only subconsciously, for the improvements you are making. This improved self-image leads to more confident actions on your part—and your ability to inspire confidence in those you lead grows as well.

Additionally, you develop a new depth of self-reliance as setting goals and making plans in different areas of life helps you deepen your self-trust. You become even more willing to commit to decisions you've made and to take the actions necessary to convert those choices into definitive results.

Developing a balanced life also heightens your level of desire and initiative. As you develop goals and plans, you build an even more passionate commitment to your own future. Your willingness to change, to take appropriate risks, and to listen to new concepts and ideas grows as a result. Greater initiative helps you take purposeful action toward the achievement of the goals you've set.

The Total Person concept inspires creativity. Indeed, no greater exercise in creativity can exist! Planning every facet of your life demands that you think "outside the box." Goal setting, by its very nature, forces you into situations in which there are no easy guidelines and few established patterns to follow. You must then devise your own path toward the achievement of your goals and your innate creativity grows as a result.

Becoming a Total Person also helps you become incredibly resilient. When you dare to be creative enough to plan your own destiny, you inevitably discover that some plans work while others do not. Rather than internalize disappointment and self-doubt, you can rely on your successes in other areas of life to rebound

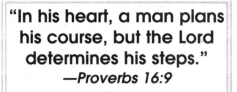

"In his heart, a man plans his course, but the Lord determines his steps."
—Proverbs 16:9

from temporary setbacks and failures. Because your creativity is in full bloom, you may find yourself devising new pathways to your goals and new solutions to the difficulties you've encountered.

Enhancing each of these qualities heightens your integrity and brings you closer to highly effective leadership. Those you lead will see you as a positive, productive role model—someone who walks the talk. Consequently, their willingness to follow your direction increases. When you explain the Total Person concept with them, they readily accept your direction because they want to be more like you.

Doing what is right

Becoming a better role model is an integral key to truly effective leadership. Your integrity calls to the integrity of your team members because the effort you are making to improve yourself has a magnetic quality. It urges those you lead to make the same effort on their own behalf. The end result: you more easily encourage, enable, and manage your followers as they move through the process of becoming committed team members.

If you are tempted by pressure, fatigue, or a slight mental let-down to compromise, avoid, back away, walk away, abandon, or discard an objective, remember that you are the role model your followers will emulate. Choosing to do what is right is often easier when you know that others are watching you.

In this case, your team members do more than just watch; they will act as you act. Your passion for integrity and achievement motivates you to do the right thing.

Chapter Six

The Third Pillar:
Passion & Desire

Truly successful leaders know the key to developing innate potential for success lies in developing a passionate desire for the development of that potential in themselves and in the members of their team as well.

Defined and refined, the goals and challenges you accept will naturally create a passion and desire for success that will not be denied. Your burning desire to achieve is the force that motivates you to do whatever it takes to get the job done.

When someone achieves an extraordinary goal, we often say, "There's a passionate individual!" When someone does something that seems not to measure up to the normal standards of dedication and commitment, we typically question the individual's passion or desire for success.

Passion and desire are the standards by which great leaders are judged, and they are the missing elements in those who vanish with time and the tide of fortune. But why are desire and passion so highly prized and why are they essential elements of highly effective leadership?

In reality, the notion that desire and passion are necessary for highly effective leaders is a vast understatement. Passion and desire are essential elements for *any* individual regardless of status or stature because they represent the ability to marshal human energy and potential and direct it toward maximum result and greatest good. Passion and desire cause undaunted enthusiasm and sureness of course. Passion and desire enable us to move forward, regardless of the personal sacrifice required or the challenge involved.

Passionate leaders see their desire for achievement as an essential extension of who they are and what they do. For the highly effective leader, passion and desire are the guiding lights that point the way toward greater success. Together, they shine as bright as beacons in the dark harbor of uncertainty, bringing inner excitement and enthusiasm to those who make decisions that affect the lives of hundreds and thousands of people. These two basic emotions and attitudes can, when properly applied, create maximum multiplication of effort for effective leaders and their followers.

> **"Life is either a daring adventure or nothing at all."**
> —*Helen Keller*

The nature of desire and passion

Highly effective leaders know that talent creates its own opportunities. Desire and passion are, in a very real sense, the catalysts and developers of talent. They combine to create their own opportunities and abilities. Effective leaders possess passion that can be transmitted to others, while desire can be learned and developed as a habit, a way of life, or a deliberate choice of a living philosophy. Once ingrained in team members and leaders, passion and desire to achieve become the source of new habits, new responses to experience, and new abilities.

This is far more than mere wanting or wishing, more than compulsion or stimulation. These elements of effective leadership represent an overwhelming inner demand for change, a personal rejection of circumstances as they are, and the willingness to make any sacrifice or bear any burden in order to bring about that change.

Every advance in history—in thought, in government, in ethics, art, religion, or science—has resulted from a single individual's desire to change the status quo, to win a race with time, with custom, tradition, or with self. This is why passion and desire burn like a flame in the heart of every effective leader. Desire is the all-important difference between winning and losing.

7 hallmarks of desire and passion

1) Desire and passion are two qualities that combine to transform average executives and managers into highly effective leaders, energized to keep working when problems cause other leaders to give up in disgust.
2) Armed with desire and passion, highly effective leaders make commitments while others make half-hearted promises.
3) Desire and passion equip highly effective leaders with the judgment and courage to say "yes" or "no" at the appropriate time; those who lack desire and passion say "maybe" at the wrong times and for the wrong reasons.
4) Desire and passion allow highly effective leaders to say, "I'm good, but not as good as I ought to be and will be." Leaders who lack desire and passion say, "I'm no worse than a lot of others."
5) Desire and passion in team members will bring respect for their leaders; lack of desire and passion can only breed resentment.
6) Desire and passion instill in highly effective leaders a strong sense of personal responsibility for more than themselves; those without desire and passion typically ask, "What's in it for me?"
7) Desire and passion are qualities to be highly prized by anyone who would become a highly effective leader. Desire and passion make success easier to attain and enhance the excitement of moving along the journey toward achievement.

The results of desire and passion

Once internalized, desire and passion produce a certain sense of restlessness and aggressiveness. Without desire and passion, leaders and organizations are tired, apathetic, and complacent. Whether desire and passion are lost through self-satisfaction or disillusionment, the absence of these qualities reveals a barren leadership future. Why? Because a future without desire and passion promises nothing better than what was offered in the past.

Highly effective leaders who possess passion and a burning desire can clearly differentiate between mature commitment to a goal and adolescent daydreaming. Desire and passion are the qualities missing in the personalities of legions of plodders and wishful thinkers. Desire and passion combine to energize leaders and followers who possess insatiable appetites for creative thinking, for action, and for achievement.

The development of desire and passion involves an active sense of self-awareness. When you know who you are and recognize the strong personal needs that cry out for satisfaction from deep within yourself, you develop an almost overwhelming sense of direction and personal purpose. You become aware that you are committed to a destiny of your own choosing; you are eager to meet and to conquer the challenges that lead to the fulfillment of that destiny.

Regardless of your current level of accomplishment, passion and desire push you to work harder. Those who lack desire often seem to be too busy to do what needs to be done. Intense desire and passion for achievement, on the other hand, point the way to exactly what is important. This is why highly effective leaders seem to know instinctively which battles to fight and when and where to compromise so they can move on to more important engagements.

Without desire and passion, nothing seems worth striving to attain. Among both leaders and team members, passion and desire for the achievement of organizational goals can produce a universal thirst for competition and success.

Indeed, aspiring leaders are often surprised to learn that passion and desire force team members to analyze themselves, to look closer at their own talents, abilities, and potential for achievement. Leaders who lack desire and passion tend to deny this introspective and competitive spirit. Typically, they devise an alibi to excuse the lack of performance from themselves and the members of their team. Others find that they have succeeded only in leveling off too soon; they must continually content themselves with less than their best.

Highly effective leaders, on the other hand, refuse to become too easily satisfied with average living and average achievements.

5 steps to developing desire and passion

To create desire and passion, successful leaders understand that they must challenge themselves and their team members. How individuals choose to react to a challenge determines their destiny. When do you challenge yourself? As a truly effective leader, you recognize that each new day brings with it the challenge:

- of a new opportunity
- to improve yesterday's record
- to compete against yourself
- to grow personally

The desire and passion with which you and your team members face a challenge is an essential part of the soul of your organization. Without it, you and your team lack spiritual guidance and creative expression. Without desire and passion, there is no intuition; missing is the still, small voice within you to provide insight into both situations and people. Without desire and passion, all of your talents and abilities tend to lie fallow and unresponsive; your potential is hidden, buried, and dormant.

If you have allowed past leadership disappointments to destroy your passion and desire, you can rebuild even greater stores of these essential qualities. Here are the 5 steps to rekindling your desire and passion:

First, strive to gain self-knowledge. Examine your innermost being. Get to know yourself, your abilities, your potential, and your needs. Know what excites and energizes you. Know what motivates you to take action. Crystallize your thinking and your objectives and clarify your own personal sense of values so that you know exactly what you believe about yourself, about life in general, and about other people. Only with adequate self-knowledge can you identify the goals that will produce enough challenge and interest to create the desire and passion you must have if you are to pursue them to achievement.

Second, make sure that the goals you set, the targets you pursue, and the rewards you desire are personally meaningful. Too often,

87

leaders and team members attempt to undertake projects or careers just to please parents, family, or others they admire. In the process, they deny their own natures and their own needs. Because their goals are not personally meaningful, they experience no internal desire to excel. They drift along, meeting minimum standards in positions they despise, never reaching the dazzling heights to which they might otherwise have aspired.

Third, work to find wisdom and knowledge in those who are in a position to advise you. Respect their insight, their special expertise, and their superior years of experience. Ponder the advice they offer, but always remember that it is your responsibility alone to make the decisions that determine the destiny of you and your team. As much as others may care for you and wish the best for you, no one else is capable of seeing into your innermost heart to understand your deepest needs and desires.

Fourth, visualize your success. Nothing increases desire and passion for achievement like controlled and directed visualization. Something unique and amazing happens when you practice looking into the future to see yourself in possession of your goals: you become so excited, so motivated, so passionate and desirous to reach them, that nothing can deter you or draw you off course.

Fifth, be willing to work harder than you've ever worked before. Work efficiently. Work long hours. Work willingly. No goal exerts enough power to produce desire and passion unless you are willing to invest much of your time and effort in bringing it to fruition. When you have invested a part of yourself in the achievement of some worthy purpose, your desire and passion know no bounds.

How to ignite passion and desire in others

Highly effective leaders are not only able to recreate the passion they feel, but they are also able to help their team members experience the same joy and excitement. Passion and desire for success, achievement, and contribution are attitudes and emotions akin to well-directed enthusiasm. Helping your team members share the passionate desire you already feel is a vital ingredient in the leadership process and will enable your team to accomplish far more than was previously possible.

Passion and desire, like enthusiasm, are sometimes misunderstood. Many leaders and managers confuse them with the mass exuberance displayed at sporting events and political conventions. But real and lasting passion and desire don't arise from temporary animation or external excitement.

Passion and desire, carefully developed and properly used, act as emotional triggers. Essentially, passion and desire are emotion management techniques—they allow you and your team members to control the emotional climate in virtually any situation. And while it is critically important that aspiring leaders and managers possess the infinite power of passionate enthusiasm, it's vital to bring it to bear with coworkers and team members as well.

As a highly effective leader, your personal success hinges upon inspiring, nurturing, cultivating, and directing the desire and passion of the members of your organization. Their passion and desire—like yours—are developed through a combination of attitudes and personal experience. Habits of thought and lessons learned by experience can contribute greatly to the development or the destruction of genuine passion.

Truly successful leaders know that the kind of effort that produces desire and passion includes: working to learn skills, developing personality traits, and acquiring the attitudes and habits required to achieve a specific goal or the organization's ultimate purpose. Highly effective leaders share this wisdom with their team members because they know that knowledge and experience come only from being active in the arena of confrontation. To develop passion, team members must be *involved* in the process of achievement.

To foster desire and passion in team members, remind them to focus on positive personal development. Specifically,

- Leaders shouldn't bemoan their lack of knowledge. *Instead, they can study and learn.*

- Leaders shouldn't complain that they have no experience. *Instead, begin to work out a plan of action to gain needed experience.*
- Leaders shouldn't worry when their first efforts seem to produce only errors. *Instead, determine to try again, and to make one fewer error every day.*
- Leaders shouldn't lament the lack of opportunity. *Opportunities abound!*
- Leaders shouldn't despair because they lack the personality traits for success. *Those traits and qualities can be developed!*

True leaders know that if they and their team members are unwilling to work to achieve organizational goals, they lack passion and desire. On the other hand, when team members and leaders push themselves into the work, passion and desire follow swiftly.

Highly effective leaders and their team members learn to welcome the adversities of life. Each of us will know we are a real success when we can face life's tests, confront its difficulties, encounter its roadblocks, and still find the courage to continue. Ideally, both leaders and followers should regard failure as a learning opportunity—a chance to try again and move closer to the target on the next attempt.

In the final analysis, desire and passion enable you and your team members to endure mistakes, misfortune, failure, and adversity—and bounce back! If you never make a mistake or experience a failure, it is probably an indication that you are not moving forward with any degree of certainty or with any sense of direction. You have probably failed to crystallize your thinking and develop plans for achievement. You have not tested your limits because you do not know where those limits lie.

Be willing to risk failure and make mistakes. Each time you venture forth to face adversity or difficulty, confront it head on and dare to take action. You are stretching your capacity a little more. Of course, you will suffer some defeats, but from each one, you and your team members will learn something new and useful. Because you move a little closer to your goal with each venture, desire and passion grow and consume you.

Evaluating desire and passion

How do efficient and effective leaders know when they have built the kind of desire and passion that will support them in achieving their objectives? The evidence is when team members have a burning desire to reach the team's goals, a passion to achieve the organization's purpose, and an overwhelming urge to help the team reach its full potential.

A young man once came to the wise philosopher Socrates and asked how to attain great wisdom. Socrates took the young man down to a river and held his head under water until he almost drowned. When he finally released the young man, Socrates asked, "What were you thinking about while your head was under water? What did you desire?"

"Air," said the youth passionately, "I wanted air!"

Socrates said, "When you want wisdom as badly as you wanted air just now, you will find wisdom."

Discerning leaders can quickly distinguish real passion and desire from wishful thinking and daydreams by asking themselves and their followers questions like these:

- What are the obstacles or roadblocks we must overcome to reach the overall goals we desire?
- What must we give in time and effort to overcome those obstacles and obtain what we desire?
- What are the rewards we will have when we have succeeded?
- Are the rewards worth what it will cost all of us in time and effort?

If you and your team answer the last question with a resounding "yes," then you can bet that desire and passion are genuine. You and your team members will be willing to do the work, expend the effort, and invest the time required to achieve your organization's goal. You will also be willing to continually resell the members of your team on making a similar commitment of time, effort, and energy. Commit yourself to taking the necessary action and your desire and passion will support you.

As passionate desire becomes an intrinsic part of your way of life, it begins in some strange and unexplainable way to use every circumstance, every contact, and every experience as a means to bring into reality the object of your desire. Desire and passion know no such word as impossible—they accept no such reality as failure.

Armed with passion and desire, you literally become a success magnet. The law of attraction is free to work for you. You begin to attract to you and your team whatever it is you need to be successful. Your enthusiasm electrifies everyone who comes in contact with you. Desire and passion combine to give you the extra energy and the extra determination to reach out for whomever and whatever you need to accomplish the job.

Highly effective leaders have found that burning desire and passion emerge when they begin to entertain great thoughts, great concepts, and great goals. When you catch a vision of greatness and crystallize your thinking about the goals you want to pursue, desire and passion flare into an eternal flame that warms, energizes, and empowers you.

Passion, desire, and rewarding leadership

It's true, becoming a successful leader requires a great deal of you. Nowhere is this more evident than in the development of passion and desire. Your intense effort is required to sustain the driving force of any passion and you are ultimately responsible for the fulfillment of your desire. But the end result of your effort can be stellar success. By developing the desire and passion necessary for effective leadership, you can create a dazzling array of opportunities to bolster your personal attitude and professional success—and the success of your organization, your team members, and your colleagues as well.

What are these opportunities for achievement?

First, you and your organization have the opportunity to provide a product or service that benefits others and improves the quality of their lives.

Second, you have the opportunity to command an honestly earned income that will fulfill the needs of your family and leave some money for luxuries and pleasure.

Third, as a highly effective leader, you have the opportunity to occupy a position of prominence that brings you acceptance and respect from team members, colleagues, and friends.

Fourth, you have the opportunity to feel fulfilled and complete when you have helped members of your team focus their desire and use more of their innate potential for success and achievement.

Fifth, you have the opportunity to find a deep satisfaction in facing challenging problems, dealing with fast-paced change, and overcoming daunting obstacles as you strive to reach the personal and professional goals you have set for yourself.

Sixth, you have the opportunity to experience the special fulfillment that comes from playing a significant part in the overall success of your organization.

Seventh, you have the opportunity to enjoy a special spirit of team pride when you realize that your efforts—and the efforts of your team members—have helped earn your organization the level of success it rightfully deserves.

Eighth, you have the opportunity to experience an even greater feeling of pride and accomplishment when the efforts of your organization render a significant service to your community and to society at large.

Committing to a standard

Highly effective leaders use their passion and desire as a springboard to propel themselves and their team members to higher levels of excellence. Vibrant, successful teams *require* passionate, desire-driven leadership. The entire organization creates an internal passion and desire for success by striving for a vision, mission, and purpose bigger than itself.

Becoming an effective, passionate leader means deciding to use your potential for success and achievement—and the innate potential of your team members—as a force for worthwhile contribution and continuous improvement. Just as you have already experienced the never-ending challenges and opportunities inherent in growing personally, so highly effective leadership gives you an unparalleled opportunity to maintain your personal and professional integrity while you contribute substantially to the lives of other people.

Highly effective leaders guide their organization through a maze of challenges, changes, and choices. It is their passion and desire that are a constant source of energy, inspiration, and direction. But sincere desire and passion are always subject to proof: to achieve the maximum degree of team productivity, highly effective leadership and passionate desire must be as evident to team members as it is to leaders who profess to practice it.

> **"It's passion probably more than anything else that separates the A's from the B's."**
> —*Jack Welch*

Chapter Seven

The Fourth Pillar:
Confidence & Trust

Great leaders are where they are and who they are because of the dominating thoughts that occupy their minds—no more and no less. Confidence and faith in their own ability to innovate, develop, persevere, and succeed are key ingredients in the success journey of any highly effective individual.

But the leadership of others implies a wider application of confidence and trust as both of these key attitudes must be extended to encompass and empower those who contribute to the overall success of the organization.

Similarly, highly effective leaders rely on self-confidence and self-trust, but developing and sharing that confidence with other members of the team can be a challenge. Why? Because developing team confidence and confidence in the team requires the creation of a unique and powerful motivational climate. Successful leaders strive to develop the trusting and empowering attitudes that are the basis for this climate.

The basis of trust and confidence

Developing *attitudes* of trust and empowerment are the first steps toward building confidence and trust among members of the team. Unfortunately, many leaders are unable to take that first step and "let go" enough to develop adequate confidence and trust in the people they manage. Others are able to delegate responsibility, but they fall short of providing the authority necessary to carry out the assignment. The most effective leaders, in contrast, are always seeking ways to enhance the capability, credibility, and potential of team members—and in so doing, they are demonstrating that trust and confidence are an integral part of what they do.

Becoming comfortable with the attitudes of confidence and trust is not an easy process for many leaders. People who start or manage a growing business are often forced at first to do almost everything themselves. There is simply no one else to help. But the day finally comes when that individual possesses neither the time nor the energy to do everything. Through the development of confidence and trust in their team members, effective leaders can multiply their own efforts again and again.

Many leaders confuse the development of confidence and trust with the routine practice of delegation, thinking that leaders who focus on confidence and trust will neither delegate nor follow up, but this could not be further from the truth. Effective leaders allow trust and confidence to make them better able to delegate.

> "This may be a networked world, but virtual trust is an illusion. Trust develops when we get to know each other. There is no substitute for spending time with people face to face."
> —James M. Kouzes & Barry Z. Posner

And if something is important enough for you to feel that you must trust someone to accomplish it, it is also important enough to require your inspection and follow-up. Does "inspecting what you expect" work to nullify confidence and trust?

Not at all—assuming that you control the *result* rather than controlling the team member. Through the development of your own trust and confidence, your team members develop their own sense of initiative and personal responsibility. Their passion for the work increases as well, and their respect for you grows because you have shown them that you have faith and confidence in their potential and ability.

Team members who deserve and demand your trust and confidence typically operate toward the same kinds of clear-cut objectives you have created for yourself and the organization. These objectives are opportunities for team members. They offer both an exciting challenge and a chance to make a valuable contribution to the overall effort.

As a highly effective leader, you can express genuine confidence and implicit trust in each team member's ability to perform successfully. You may even offer to teach a particular process or procedure first before gradually letting go of the work. In this way, trust and confidence work together to allow highly effective leaders to empower team members with the responsibility for the achievement of an important objective.

Empowerment and levels of trust

As you develop your leadership role, make every effort to offer trust to virtually every member of your organization. Trust is the key to personal empowerment; if you withhold it, you hamper that individual's ability to grow and develop personally. If you have a legion of team members waiting to do something until you give them explicit instructions, you waste both your time and the potential of the team.

Trust and confidence, on the other hand, empower team members to seek your direction or approval and then proceed with the task. Your ability to communicate objectives and clarify assignments, coupled with your inspection of the work and a rudimentary tracking system, will go a long way toward helping team members take action and routinely report to you with their results.

The best leaders develop trust in their team members by tapping into the attitudes and values of each individual. This is the key to nurturing commitment and accountability in the goal directed team. How your team members view their work produces a significant impact on long-term productivity and offers you important feedback about their ability to perform to your expectations.

Confident leaders can boost their level of trust by adopting attitudes conducive to organizational productivity. Thinking and talking in terms of "we" or "us," not just "me" or "I," is a good start. Effective leaders should also recognize that mistakes are simply a part of the learning process and imply nothing about the value, worth, or potential of the team member responsible. Indeed, leaders who recognize that team members learn through mistakes and repetition will often replace the word "failure" with words like "learning experience" or "trial."

Additionally, the most successful leaders are always available for their team members. Effective leaders offer credit for contributions to organizational success and help devise ways to keep problems from reoccurring. Their willingness to trust the members of their team sends an important message: "Do whatever it takes to get the job done. I'm confident that you have the talent to succeed!"

Many effective leaders will not always trust that each task will be completed to perfection in a timely manner, but they do always trust every team member to develop and use more of his or her unique potential for achievement.

How to develop the potential of team members

If leaders are to develop their own levels of team member trust and confidence, understanding how their team members grow personally is essential. Personal growth and development is more than the mere process of learning; it implies expression of new knowledge and skills in the quest to achieve a worthwhile goal.

While your team members may express acquired knowledge in many different ways, the process of gathering and expressing new concepts and ideas is quite straightforward and it applies to virtually every member of your organization. Simply stated, individuals absorb new information, tailor it to fit their own preconceptions, and express it in a way that fulfills their own needs and the needs of the team as well.

This means that knowledge, behavior, attitudes, and values are all acquired through a process we described years ago as "mental osmosis." Of course, people are not born with ingrained or specific attitudes. Instead, those habits of thought are caused, created, and instilled by outside forces. From the moment of birth, all of us engage in a process of acquiring information, relating that information to our environment, and expressing newfound concepts and ideas to others around us. As a consequence of the information we absorb, we develop and change our attitudes and behaviors.

By adulthood, our attitudes—toward life, toward work, toward other people—have largely shaped our values, which are the standards by which we judge the people and events that surround us. And, by the time we reach adulthood, our behavior is controlled largely by habit. In fact, nearly all daily adult activity is performed via habit.

If leaders at every level wish to develop a high level of confidence and trust in the attitudes and work habits of their team members, they must:

- offer new and personally meaningful ideas and information
- help team members relate these new concepts to their own situation
- work with team members to develop new habits and attitudes that incorporate the new ideas

How do team members decide what information to absorb and retain? How do they determine what they will pay attention to? Both knowledge and intelligence are acquired through a process involving curiosity and interest. Small children are fascinated by virtually everything; they acquire knowledge and information at a phenomenal rate, but curiosity wanes as youngsters move through the first years of the educational process. Finally, it becomes difficult—if not impossible—to interest a young person in any given subject. This is because their curiosity has largely been destroyed by the need to conform to the standards of the society into which they are attempting to integrate themselves.

This need to conform also helps shape and determine adult behavior in the world of work. Behavior is the recurring inclination to react in a certain way each time you encounter a particular circumstance or situation. Individuals often allow old behaviors to limit their progress purely because their behavior is comfortable or they do not realize the limiting nature of the way they act.

Anyone who has ever worked with teenagers has almost certainly tapped into the powerful urge to conform. A few young leaders on a team or in a class can greatly influence their peers toward achievement. By creating positive peer pressure and tapping into the need to conform, leaders at every level can create a more stimulating and challenging learning environment.

If the need to conform is too strong, however, individuals cannot grow. If it is not strong enough, chaos reigns rather than order. To establish the correct need to conform, highly effective leaders offer new attitudes, new values, and new, easily assimilated behaviors.

The power of attitude formation

Like ingrained behaviors, attitudes are habits—habits of thought. They are formed in the same way as habits of behavior or action. When a particular type of thought or thought pattern gives you some sort of mental satisfaction, you repeat it. Eventually, it becomes a habit of thought—an attitude.

Attitudes are thoughts that, through repetition and the process of visualization, have become ingrained in the mind of the individual who holds them. While behaviors—habits of action—are usually formed by attempting several different courses of action and then choosing the most satisfactory one, attitudes tend to require more concrete footing.

We all test habits of thought by mentally associating ourselves with past experiences. In similar situations, we are able to recall the thought almost at will and repeat it again and again.

Attitudes are formed and rest upon a foundation of values. Our values determine what we pay attention to and they dictate our habits of thought. *It is difficult—if not impossible—to change someone's attitudes without first restructuring the values that are essential building blocks of those new attitudes.* Preconceptions and experiences of early childhood contribute to value formation. Attitudes are then tightly tied to the values that are at the deepest roots of our being. Uprooting old values in an effort to "trade" for more appropriate values requires us to first address the underlying conditioning. But unless new conditioning replaces the old, values will typically remain the same.

For decades, leaders have expected team members to magically develop value systems congruent with their own. Leaders and managers have tried to create new attitudes through efforts to educate followers and change their behavior. The vital missing link—values—has been largely ignored.

The reason is simple: many leaders have been trained to look for the quick fix. By modifying how someone acts within the organizational setting or by modifying the organizational setting itself, leaders expected to modify that individual's value system. But while behavior may be altered, values and the resulting habits of thought typically remain the same! Until the core values are changed, the attitudes remain largely inflexible. In the final analysis, long-term change never really takes place.

The most successful leaders are able to engineer value changes by helping their team members develop new, more positive conditioning and attitudes about themselves, their colleagues, the organization, team objectives, and society in general. This new conditioning, once ingrained, builds the altered value systems that produce and spur self-motivation and other productive habits of thought. Values inevitably change as attitudes and conditioning are transformed.

The most significant transformation takes place as team members acquire a more positive self-image. That self-image, in turn, is recreated again and again through the development of trust and confidence, and this is where the power originates to cause long-term positive change.

The dynamics of personal development

Understanding how your team members grow and improve brings to light something called the "results continuum." Put simply, the continuum serves as a template for any accomplishment. Just as attitudes cannot be altered without first changing the underlying values, so the results all of us seek are dependent upon specific action, which in turn is driven by habits of thought, and habits of thought are created via specific input.

In fact, any result begins with some kind of input. Curiosity is aroused, knowledge is shared, and something must go through the mental process before any viable result can be produced. This means that the input must stir something in the imagination or spirit that brings the mechanism of conscious thought into play.

Input comes from both without and within. In most work situations, input is directed to the individual from others on the team or from someone in a position of leadership. Leaders require input as well, but typically they have fewer people to offer it. This means that leaders probably tend to create more mental input on their own since it does not come from someone else. Like the development of behaviors and attitudes, every individual produces some of his or her own mental input.

However, acquiring the ability to produce your own input and block out the negative input of others can take time and practice. You may have discovered this fundamental truth yourself!

Positive or negative input?

The ideal input, from the perspective of a successful leader, revolves around goals and objectives that contribute to the development of each team member. Effective leaders strive to ensure that the majority of the input they offer focuses on what is conducive to the development of goals in the various areas of life.

Unfortunately, many leaders are, often out of necessity, too focused on immediate results and short-term goals. As a result, they offer input that deals almost exclusively with behavior modification and skill-oriented information. Any real input dealing with the team member personally is scanty at best, totally absent at worst.

This is because many leaders and managers have become susceptible to negative input from other people. This tendency demonstrates itself in the way they deal with the members of their team. Highly effective leaders, on the other hand, recondition themselves and their attitudes to become perceptive to the positive input of other people. These two simple definitions understate the importance of focus and attitude.

If effective leaders are to build effective organizations, they first are required to accept the fact that skill building and task-oriented input will produce mostly superficial change and almost no substantive result. Successful leaders, then, strive for long-term change through providing input that will help team members continue to develop and grow personally.

Input produces conscious thought and thought is the basic building block of actions and results. Seldom does anything happen without conscious thought. Of course, we've all heard stories of heroic feats performed without the hero having given much thought to the task. Someone who lifts an automobile off of an injured person can hardly be expected to be thinking about the process beforehand. Indeed, in such circumstances, thinking ahead of the task would probably rob the individual of the ability to perform it.

Such occurrences are the rare exception. In almost all situations, conscious thought is required before action can take place. And, just as investment precedes dividend, so action is the precursor of results.

Getting to results

Action is the required element in the results continuum...nothing happens without it. It is entirely possible for someone to receive input and generate thought without taking action on the thought. In leading and managing people, you may actually see this happening on a daily basis.

To generate action and produce an appropriate result, both input and thought must be sufficient to blast the individual out of the lethargy that is the natural product of mental or physical inactivity. A law of physics comes into play here: the body or mind at rest tends to stay at rest. Unless the input and the thought process work together to prod the individual into action, a result is never generated.

Does this mean that the result should no longer be considered the be-all and end-all of any process of achievement? Yes and no. The result is certainly important because nothing happens until some result is produced, but the process of creating the result can give leaders powerful insight into just what is required for the processes of achievement and self-improvement. The real benefit of the results continuum is to teach us the steps we must take before we have a legitimate right to expect specific outcomes.

Infinite needs, infinite resources

In an ordinary organization, needs beget needs. In a highly effective organization, needs fulfill needs by enlisting the untapped potential of team members. On the surface, however, this seems paradoxical at best. How can a need, a want, or a desire actually serve to fulfill another need?

The answer lies in the desire of people to become more than they are and in the striving of individuals on your team to contribute to both their individual goals and the overall objectives of the organization.

Think for a moment about how needs beget needs in an ordinary organization. The need for more office space creates the need for more expansion capital. The need for expansion capital begets the need for additional product sales. The need for more product sales spurs the need for more production. The need for more production fosters the need for more efficient and effective workers. Needs give birth to other needs in a never-ending cycle of progress, growth, and change.

But effective leaders recognize that resources are infinite. Workers, in an effort to fulfill their own needs and the needs of the team, have the potential to increase their production. Salespeople have the ability to increase their sales—after all, they have more product to sell. Increased sales produce a surplus of expansion capital, and some of that money can then be used to develop additional office space. The process continues, ad infinitum, purely because we think about the prospects of plentiful surplus rather than dwell upon limitation after limitation.

This critical attitude—this "no-limitations" habit of thought— is an essential building block for highly effective leaders. Leaders who lead with an expectancy of limitation will always fail because the needs they create and dwell upon only create additional needs. If your company is in debt, for instance, focusing your thoughts on the debt will only fasten your debt more tightly about you. Dwelling on negatives, failings, and lack will never improve the situation you face—a different habit of thought is required.

Leaders who manage with a no-limitations belief in themselves and their team members will find that the needs they help create do indeed fulfill other needs. The process moves from a chain of distraction and dissatisfaction to one of contentment and ever-expanding prosperity. Focusing on the possibilities is called "possibility thinking" and allows leaders to use a need itself to point the way to solutions. This is the essence of needs-directed leadership.

Seeing the positive nature of needs fulfilling needs may well be the ultimate test of effective leadership. Few ordinary leaders and managers can see the needs of their organization in anything but an ambivalent or slightly negative light. Their myopic vision is induced by pressure to produce and provide for the needs themselves.

Highly effective leaders, on the other hand, work to transmit the positive expectancy of needs fulfilling needs to each member of their team. A pervasive needs-fulfill-needs philosophy clearly defines and immeasurably strengthens the attitudes and values of the effective organization.

What team member needs can an effective organization fulfill? In the family and home area of life, the team can offer support, counsel, and camaraderie. For goals dealing with finances and career, the organization offers the opportunity to advance in rank and position and to grow financially. In the spiritual and ethical area of life, members of the organization can provide comfort and spirit-filled kinship from like-minded individuals. Socially and culturally, team members may provide friends, companions, and individuals with whom to share some of life's pleasures. In the mental and educational area, the organization provides opportunities to learn and grow, even if only to acquire a new skill. For goals in the physical and health area, the organization can offer some sort of health care program or insurance, and committed leaders can help team members in their quest to achieve challenging physical goals.

It's fair to say that teams and organizations that do not support team members' personal goals actually create unfulfilled needs among those individuals. This is the central reason why workplace environments continue to deteriorate. Until leaders take the time to become whole themselves and to establish some semblance of an effective organization, needs go unfulfilled. The end result, of course, is more of what we have become accustomed to seeing in the workplace: continued deterioration of our enterprise, our community, and society.

Developing the highly effective team

You are an effective leader when you have successfully developed an effective team—a group of followers comprised of individuals who, like yourself, are actively pursuing objectives in all areas of life. Building your effective team will take time. How much time the process will take will depend largely upon how many team members you lead, how quickly you can develop your own trust and confidence, and how intensive you choose to make the process of personal growth and organizational achievement.

When does the effective team cross the line to become an effective organization? There are really three answers to that question:

First, an effective organization is developed by effective work teams (note the plural form!). Each team within the organization must be made up of individuals who are committed to growing personally—and to growing the organization as well.

Second, an effective team becomes an effective organization when the team members begin to give something back to the community they share and inhabit. Every community has specific and immediate needs—needs that can be fulfilled by members of the effective team. Effective teams are staffed with members of the organization who themselves have a need to make a contribution—a need that is usually fulfilled by giving something back. Your effective team crosses the line to committed organization status when they begin to contribute something to others, to community organizations, and to the common welfare.

Third, an effective organization is born when members of effective teams are convinced enough of the validity of leadership that they are willing to openly declare their trust, respect, and admiration for effective leaders. This doesn't mean that your team members must worship the ground upon which you walk. Far from it. All of us have feet of clay—none of us are perfect—but your quest to become a successful leader is incredibly shallow and probably less than genuine if your team members cannot come to respect and admire you for your willingness to pursue objectives in all areas of life.

If you believe that nothing can give you that kind of appreciation and goodwill among those you lead, you are selling yourself short. Heretofore, members of your team may not have expressed those qualities because they did not believe you were sincerely interested in their welfare and improvement, or that you had confidence and trust in their ability to succeed. In the process of becoming a highly effective leader, your faith and trust go a long way toward eradicating that attitude.

In search of belief, confidence, and trust

If you wish to bridge the leadership gap effectively and you recognize that you can do that only through confidence in yourself and belief in your team members' abilities, then your path is set. Becoming a confident, trusting leader takes time, because learning to have confidence and trust in yourself and others is not a rapid process. In the instant-gratification, quick-fix world that is modern management, you may feel that developing confidence in your team members is a task that can be postponed.

Unfortunately, it doesn't work that way. You cannot propose to help others climb to the pinnacle of personal and team success if you are unwilling to increase your own ability to trust them. Your effort to transform others without transforming yourself is tantamount to going back to somewhere you have never been. Most likely, you will succeed only in destroying the little bit of confident, trusting leadership you have already worked hard to create. Your team members will lose their belief in you, in your integrity, and in your ability to effectively lead and mange them to greater achievement.

Confident, trusting leadership is no management fad; it is a way of life. It may take you a hundred days...or a thousand...but you must strive to make trust and confidence in others an integral part of your personality before you can inspire or require it in someone else.

Remember Spartacus!

Can you measure up to the standards of a worthy leader? There is one way to find out—you can strive to emulate someone who undoubtedly was a trusting, confident, and worthy leader. In fact, it could be argued that Spartacus' followers died to prove his leadership status!

Perhaps you know the story of Spartacus. As a young adult, he was the leader of a band of robbers; hardly an appropriate occupation for a highly effective leader! He and his followers suffered the misfortune of being captured and sold to a gladiator trainer. In 73 B.C., Spartacus escaped and took about seventy followers with him. They hid in the crater of the volcano Vesuvius and hordes of runaway slaves joined the band.

Spartacus became the leader of a great insurrection of Roman slaves and he and his band eventually took control of much of southern Italy. Rome sent army after army against him, but Spartacus defeated the legions. His concern for his followers was the stuff of legend; he was fighting for a better life for them all. But it was not to be.

In 71 B.C., two years after the rebellion had begun, the Roman Emperor Crassus managed to crush the insurrection and Spartacus was killed in a last great battle. But the Romans didn't know Spartacus was dead; they believed the slave leader was still alive and hidden among his followers.

Without exception, every follower of Spartacus took up the mantle of their fallen leader. In response to intense Roman questioning, each former slave proudly proclaimed, "I am Spartacus!" The Romans had no way of knowing who among the hundreds of slaves was telling the truth and who might be Spartacus. Frustrated and enraged, the Romans crucified them all.

What if the Romans came knocking at your door today? How would your followers respond? Would they betray you and your mission? Or would they respect you enough and believe in your cause enough to risk something of themselves in your name?

When you can have sincere trust and confidence that your followers would unhesitatingly make a personal sacrifice in your behalf, you will know that the fourth pillar—Confidence & Trust—in your leadership bridge is firmly planted in a bedrock that will not be moved.

> **"Trust men and they will be true to you. Trust them greatly and they will show themselves great."**
> —*Ralph Waldo Emerson*

You are well on your way to building a bridge of leadership that will span the test of time.

Chapter Eight

The Fifth Pillar:
Commitment & Responsibility

Here's a simple formula that can eliminate 90 percent of all the failures you and your team members will ever experience: ***don't quit!*** Quitting is the #1 reason why people fail to reach a particular objective or to achieve a meaningful goal.

Unfortunately, the individuals on your team who give up or quit trying are typically just as capable as you or anyone else to succeed. They lack just a few important success attitudes that can actually be cultivated and acquired quickly and easily.

How much do you want it?

It stands to reason that most individuals who give up before achieving a goal never had a white-hot, burning desire to succeed. The intensity of that desire, in large measure, determines the effective boundaries of an individual's potential for achievement. The greater the desire, the greater the success potential. Desire is a jealous suitor; it leaves no room for thoughts of quitting.

You already know that in order to cultivate desire in your team members you must build upon the first leadership pillar—Crystallized Thinking. Crystallized thinking is the first essential element of desire. Unless goals are the product of crystallized thinking, it is all too easy for a team member to quit at the first hint of trouble. Intense desire cannot be created unless goals have been clearly defined.

111

Of course, hazy goals lack the sharp focus that allows you and your team members to concentrate your full attention and energy on their achievement. Unfocused concentration does not make someone efficient in a number of different areas; instead, it serves to add an element of mental confusion. The inevitable result is a diluted, dissipated personal power and a random scattering of personal energy.

Even those leaders who have an abundant desire to be a great leader may find themselves giving up if they lack commitment (commitment is defined: *it is done*). Commitment focuses any leader's entire being on the goal that must be accomplished and is the measure of your team members' willingness to keep working toward specific goals regardless of the difficulties they might face.

> "When anyone tells me I can't do anything, I'm just not listening anymore."
> —*Florence Joyner*

In a way, modern technology has done us a disservice by teaching us to expect everything to be instantly available. Instant food, instant drinks, instant cash, instant credit, you name it, we want it instantly. Because we have become accustomed to instant gratification, many of us get upset if that pattern of immediate gratification changes.

This is the core reason behind the willingness of many people—perhaps some of your own team members—to give up at the first sign of difficulty or delay. Fortunately, effective leaders know that important goals cannot be achieved instantly. They require:

- time
- planning
- effort
- dedication

Giving up quickly is the worst possible tragedy. Leaders at every level must understand that they cannot allow lack of patience, lack of persistence, or lack of commitment to be responsible for missing the achievement of an important goal or objective.

The reality of the situation is this: whenever you encounter a difficulty or a problem in the pursuit of a goal, you are free either to keep working toward the objective or to quit. Your team members, whether you realize it or not, have the same choices. Those who want to succeed—the real winners among your colleagues—will never abandon the goal, no matter what happens. They will stay with the task, remaining faithful to your purpose, no matter how much work or hardship is involved and in spite of what other team members might say, think, or do.

The 4 elements of persistence

The desire to succeed and the commitment to reach significant goals combine to create persistence. Persistence makes the difference over time between winning and losing, between success and failure, and is comprised of these 4 key elements:

Element #1—raw determination, which is the refusal to give up, to quit, or to be defeated. Determination is a result of the confidence created by written and specific goals. Individuals who lack a detailed understanding of where they want to go and why they want to go there will never feel secure about their goals. Because they have failed to fully crystallize their thinking, they never really know whether the goals they've chosen are correct! Armed with a clear, concise plan of action, effective leaders and team members feel secure enough to push ahead. They know that their efforts will pay off handsomely in the end.

Element #2—patience to willingly keep at a job, task, or goal despite temporary setbacks and encroaching difficulties. Mature people are usually willing to work now in exchange for a future reward. That is why many leaders and team members are able to work toward an important goal over a long period of time. They receive their present satisfaction—the mental reward that motivates them to keep on going—through their anticipation of the actual reward that follows. In a very real sense, persistence *requires* patience.

Leaders who have crystallized their thinking and developed written plans for the achievement of their goals find that persistence is a natural consequence of the planning process. That's because no goal, no matter how massive or minute, can be accomplished in reality before it has been accomplished mentally.

Element #3—a justifiable sense of pride for using more of your full potential for success. Of course, this kind of pride is unrelated to the boastful arrogance often displayed by those who substitute words for actions. For you and your team members, pride in winning is evidenced by your quiet, internal satisfaction, in knowing that each of you has contributed the best effort possible and that the resulting achievement is both significant and worthwhile.

Element #4—a willingness to take appropriate risks in order to ensure the achievement of a goal. Despite your best efforts to crystallize your thinking and develop a plan for success, it is not always possible to predict with surety the end result of a particular course of action. Willingness to take appropriate risks is evidenced by leaders and team members who apply imagination and ingenuity to devise new solutions to challenging problems.

Winning leaders and their team members possess the courage necessary to attempt previously untried solutions. Those who like to "play it safe" are undoubtedly missing opportunities to move toward their goals.

The development of persistence—like any other success quality— is a little like becoming an alcoholic. Taking many separate drinks can eventually produce an addiction to alcohol that seems almost impossible to break. Just as the alcoholic must have another drink, so one who has tasted the wine of success once must taste it again...and again...and again. Successful thoughts and actions are just as addictive as the more negative aspects of our society.

Persistence becomes a habit of thought through the continuing practice of the attitudes and behaviors that lead to success. With enough repetition, the attitude of persistence becomes almost automatic. Those who have acquired a persistent attitude in this way seem never to think of giving up. Somehow, they automatically keep on going...and going...until the particular goal has been achieved.

In the final analysis, persistence is born of crystallized thinking, built upon detailed plans for achievement of goals, backed by desire and confidence, and grounded in commitment.

Finding uses for adversity

Many leaders and followers buckle quickly under the onslaught of adversity. They lack true staying power, even though they possess tremendous potential and challenging dreams. Successful leaders and their team members, on the other hand, are thankful for adversity because in every adversity is the seed of a greater or at least equivalent benefit.

Effective leaders rely upon adversity to call up the best that is within them. When you face adversity, determined to conquer and overcome it, you are literally forced to use more of your full potential for achievement. Using your vivid imagination, you develop new strategies for overcoming problems and reaching your goal. Your efforts intensify because you begin to exercise an even greater level of personal initiative. Adversity is the ultimate act of disclosure—it reveals to you the full depth of your potential, the full force of your power, and the broad spectrum of your talents and abilities.

Adversity, difficulty, and temporary defeat are stepping stones in disguise—stepping-stones to greater success and achievement. Problems or setbacks cause effective leaders to react in new and different ways. These individuals also grow personally at a faster rate than might be possible were circumstances easier. The best leaders among us are sincerely grateful for the obstacles that serve to test the commitment of themselves (and their team members) and for the difficulties that demand the best of every member of the organization.

A problem-solving plan

All leaders face difficulties, and, at some time or another, all leaders become discouraged. Instead of giving in, develop a plan for handling the problem. First, write out a list of four or five reasons why

115

you are thankful that you have been given the problem. Of course, this requires some degree of persistence because thinking of five reasons for being thankful for adversity isn't always easy to do!

Your list might include reasons like these:

- I'm thankful I did not face this obstacle five years ago when I didn't have as much knowledge and experience as I have now
- I'm grateful I discovered this difficulty in ample time to work to correct the problem before it can cause irreparable damage
- I'm glad that, over the past few years, I've built relationships of trust and respect with many of my team members in our organization; I am confident that I can call on them for effort and advice in this challenging situation
- I'm grateful that the creativity I use and the effort I expend in the process of overcoming this obstacle will demonstrate to my colleagues and team members that I am the kind of individual who can help them develop and use more of their own potential for achievement

Examining your list, you may be struck by the thought that every obstacle or difficulty really holds a benefit that you might miss if you do not work through the problem. Your list of reasons becomes objective evidence of personal gain. The exciting challenge before you is the task of finding the best way around, through, or over the roadblock you've encountered.

Those who have never struggled with difficulty can never know the full joy of success. At any level of leadership, the real thrill of success comes from realizing that, by your own persistence and effort, you have averted or eluded failure.

Of course, you and your team members are completely free to choose how you will react to adversity. You can allow difficulty to defeat you, or you can see obstacles as opportunities to use more of your collective potential.

Truly great leaders adamantly reject the dire warnings of negative thinkers who point out the possibility of error, who offer continuing discouragement, or who doubt the potential of effective leadership.

Great leaders listen, instead, to their inner voice of confidence and determination. They create that inner voice by searching for ways to achieve their goals—and not for excuses to quit.

Courage to dream

Effective leaders understand that qualities like imagination, creativity, and potential for success become useful only when they are put to work to achieve a meaningful goal. An integral part of this actualization process involves learning to dream, to use imagination and creative power in ways that will produce specific goals for themselves and their team members.

But it takes courage to dream. The moment you generate a creative idea, you become a minority of one. You stand alone until others can be persuaded to join in pursuit of your dream. Even then you will be the only individual who has a singular depth of belief and commitment to the dream.

For many team members, the ability to dream may have been almost completely destroyed by negative past experiences. During childhood, the process of conditioning robs many of us of the ability to dream. Teachers and parents may deliver stern admonitions to quit daydreaming and get to work; the child then infers that any attempt to crystallize or visualize the future is somehow a wasted effort. Similarly, many of your team members may have acquired the belief that wanting anything—for any reason—is somehow selfish and wrong.

The sad consequence of these childhood experiences is the large percentage of adults who have lost their ability to dream. Before leaders and team members can reach the level of success they desire and deserve, they must first rid themselves

> **Leaders bear the responsibility of sharing the necessity for dreaming with team members who may lack the courage to visualize greater achievement.**

of the notion that dreaming and yearning is wasted effort or selfish greed.

But discarding these old beliefs, whether in a family environment or in the world of work, is not always easy. That is why team members should be encouraged to use their creativity, no matter how damaged or dormant it might be. Each member of your organization deserves to possess their dreams if they are willing to pursue them and work diligently to bring them into reality. Personal success is not reserved for the leadership elite; everyone deserves to enjoy it. But success begins with dreaming—and dreaming requires courage.

Courage to face yourself

Some leaders manage to find the courage to dream and imagine, but they lack the mental fortitude to "face themselves" (acknowledge their own weaknesses, draw on their own strengths, and analyze where they stand now in relation to where they want to go). We all have elements of personality or personal habits with which we are not entirely pleased. Of course, it is tempting to deny that these personality characteristics or personal traits even exist, but such a course leads only to complacency. Without the courage to face yourself, all your dreams fade into meaningless fantasies; nothing will ever come of them.

As a leader, you should exercise the courage necessary to make a fair assessment of your own personal resources. This assessment should paint a realistic picture of where you stand now in relation to your own personal and professional journey. While you may not be entirely satisfied with what you learn about yourself, you cannot afford to feel discouraged.

The strengths and weaknesses you have developed at this point in your personal journey are completely unrelated to your worth as a human being or to your potential for highly effective leadership. *Your assessment is information about past growth, not your future potential.* Many leaders have never given a great deal of thought to the process of self-knowledge and self-examination; the process may feel vaguely uncomfortable to them. Of course, new or unknown situations are always somewhat frightening, but self-knowledge is a tool that allows leaders and team members to take control of their future, to command their own destiny.

118

Courage to start

As you know, the basic law of physics states that a body at rest tends to remain at rest. This law is responsible for a simple leadership fact—***the quality most crucial to attaining success for yourself and your organization is the courage to begin!***

It requires more power to take off in an airplane than it does to just keep going. More force is required to change direction than to proceed in a straight line. This law works in your organization as well. If you and your team members are sitting back and waiting for your proverbial ship to come in, you'll find it incredibly easy to keep on sitting there! Circumstances will never drop dreams into your lap. The longer you sit back and wait, the more dynamite will be required to blast you and your organization into productive action.

Overcoming inertia requires the greatest amount of energy and courage. Once you and your organization are in motion, another law of physics works in your favor: a body in motion tends to stay in motion. Sheer momentum will help you keep moving.

Courage to risk

Without risks, no leader can become truly great. Why? Because no real progress can be achieved, no new product created, and no new innovations championed without some degree of risk. And without courage, leaders take no risks.

The feeling of security is a basic human need. In their broadest sense, security and safety can be threatened by almost any departure from the present norm. If your dream is to introduce a new product line, risks to your security are somewhat obvious. While you will probably not be in any physical danger, there is the danger that the new product line might not be successful. Loss of income and investment capital could create financial difficulties for your organization, your friends and colleagues might call you foolhardy, and your banker might even refuse to back you with needed financial resources.

Certainly, reaching for the stars is a risky business, but your failure to take those risks sets up an even more dangerous risk—the possibility that you and your team will miss the chance to fulfill dreams, to develop potential and ability, and to achieve goals that best express fulfillment of your purpose.

The source of leadership courage

How you respond to the challenges and decisions you face is not just a matter of your personal choice—it is the defining moment of your leadership experience. Any leader can retreat in fear; only the most effective leaders can instinctively push forward with courage, conviction, and determination.

The choice is yours to make. This is not to say that the choice is easy. For the effective leader, the courage to make the choice comes from deep within. Leaders who possess courage also possess the qualities necessary to help themselves and their team members become more than they are.

Among leaders, no choice is more difficult than deciding to act with courage and conviction. But once leaders push themselves to act courageously in a single area of life or in one aspect of their business role, it becomes progressively easier to act with courage in other areas and in other situations.

Unfortunately, leaders must realize that no one can have courage for them. Effective leaders *consciously* choose courage as an option. As a leader, you open up new pathways to your objectives when you choose to act with courage. You discover new depths of resources and potential within yourself and your team members.

The buck stops here!

The plaque on President Harry Truman's desk read, "The Buck Stops Here!" He understood that he bore the weight of important decisions. Today, virtually every leader shoulders some element of responsibility for outcomes. The burden you bear may not be as great as was Truman's, but the same sentiment still applies. As a leader, you are the responsible party. For initiatives you design or approve, for policies and procedures you develop or implement, and for projects you oversee or champion, the buck stops with you.

Accept the fact that nothing—*absolutely nothing*—you do in your organization will produce the successful results you desire until you as a leader choose to accept personal responsibility for what happens to you and your colleagues.

The blame game

Unfortunately, many people are accustomed to blaming others for their own shortcomings. Children blame their parents, students blame their teachers, employees blame their employer, criminals blame society or their victims, and all of us, at one time or another, blame the government!

When we expend energy and time blaming others for our own failures and for who we are as individuals, there is less energy left for growth, improvement, and success. Blaming others, reliving past failures, and repeating mistakes over and over again are merely ways leaders and followers have devised to avoid accepting personal responsibility for their actions.

Leaders who accept personal responsibility for who they are also recognize: their own knowledge of past mistakes and failures, their own admission of personality faults and negative habit patterns, and their own understanding of the powerful negative conditioning that has brought them to this point *are merely items of information!* All these things combine to tell effective leaders where to start on the road to achieving the true success of which they are capable.

> **You alone are responsible for what you can become.**

Indeed, the failures of the past are significant only if you repeat them or refuse to learn from them. Although parents, teachers, and society in general may truly deserve some of the credit or blame for who you are today, you alone are responsible for what you can become.

Not only must you, as a leader, accept personal responsibility for who you are, but you must also accept personal responsibility for your feelings and emotions as well.

If you find yourself feeling afraid, hesitant, or discouraged, recognize that no one but you is responsible for the fact that you are experiencing a negative emotion.

The simple fact is that no person and no outside circumstance can make you feel any particular way. Your team members and events can certainly contribute to situations that create various emotions, but how you feel about those situations is, in the final analysis, your own personal choice.

When leaders refuse to let the actions and words of others affect their attitude, they exhibit the kind of maturity that allows them to take charge of their own lives—and this same maturity goes a long way toward convincing team members and colleagues that their leader truly holds their best interests close to heart.

Accepting responsibility for leadership actions

Once you accept personal responsibility for who you are and how you feel, the next logical step is the acceptance of personal responsibility for the actions you take. When leaders accept personal responsibility for their actions, they avoid comparing themselves to others. They evaluate their own actions against a standard—the standard of personal and organizational goals that will measure their own excellence.

Such leaders have no need to judge their performance by a clock; they don't quit for the day just because they have fulfilled the minimum daily requirements for keeping the doors open. Armed with personal responsibility, effective leaders go the extra mile to keep their commitments to themselves, to their team members, and to their customers.

You may have noticed that highly effective leaders often exceed the best that others expect of them. This is because these individuals have made a habit of rising to meet needs as they become aware of them. They understand that the one leadership factor with the largest potential for outstanding success is their willingness to take personal responsibility for the organization they lead.

The benefits of personal responsibility

In the area of personal and organizational growth, you have a magnificent opportunity to seize personal responsibility and exercise it for greater good. As an effective leader, you can experience unusual personal growth both as an individual and as a businessperson.

And, in a very real sense, you become a merchant of personal growth and success for those with whom you work. The product you are selling—the personal habits and behavior characteristics that lead to the achievement of individual and organizational dreams—is the same product you've used yourself. Because you have become a product of that product through dreaming great dreams, making noble plans, and daily pursuing them, those around you will be able to sense your personal growth and want to experience the same thing in their own lives.

But personal and professional growth is always a choice. Just as you cannot force team members to become more than they are, so no one can force you to grow. You must ask yourself: "Am I willing to pay the price to accept the responsibility for personal growth?"

Think well on your answer. Your iron-willed determination to succeed hinges upon your decision to accept personal responsibility for your own personal development. The trust that you place in others will be strengthened or shattered by your decision to grow personally or to stay the way you are. The desire to achieve new and significant goals will be dramatically increased or reduced to nil, depending on your decision. The dreams you've dreamed and the plans you've made all rely on accepting personal responsibility for progress, growth, and change.

While the result of accepting personal responsibility is the true freedom to become what your Creator destined you to be, the real benefit is the success you vividly imagine, ardently desire, sincerely believe, and enthusiastically act upon.

What happens without responsibility?

Some other leaders have refused to accept personal responsibility and have fallen into apathy and bondage. *This fate must not befall you!*

Other leaders have rejected personal responsibility and have failed miserably. *Their failure must not become yours!*

Others have feared personal responsibility and have thus allowed incredible opportunities to slip through their grasp. *Their loss must not be your loss!*

Still others have neglected to accept personal responsibility and have drifted into the depths of mediocrity. *Their waste of potential and ability must be theirs alone!*

The acceptance of personal responsibility is a way of living that stands as an ideal for yourself, for your organization, for our nation, for whole societies, and for the entire planet.

Why? Because when free people dare to accept personal responsibility for themselves and for their own lives, they bring incredible freedom for achievement to the organizations to which they contribute. And one person at a time, they bring freedom to the entire human race.

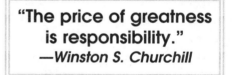

"The price of greatness is responsibility."
—Winston S. Churchill

Leaders must accept personal responsibility for their own success and failure. By taking an appropriate risk, you expand your own capabilities. This too is a freedom—the freedom of leaders and followers to reach within themselves, find the potential placed there by their Creator, and use that potential to grow, achieve, and fulfill the purpose for which they were created.

Chapter Nine

Leadership at
the Crossroads

Progress, growth, and change are the order of humanity. Truly great leaders embrace change with open arms because they know and understand that without change, nothing survives.

Change is an integral part of life—and it is just as much an integral part of leadership. After all, if nothing ever changed, leadership would be a simple process of putting working procedures into place and watching them operate. But change is inevitable, which makes leadership largely the challenge of managing it.

Everyone responds differently to change—some are frightened, depressed, or even paralyzed, incapable of taking action of any kind. Others see change as the challenge that it is—they are inspired, energized, and revitalized.

Leaders can neither prevent nor avoid change. It roars along like a mighty river, but it is a river that can be properly channeled and utilized as a driving force for achievement.

3 keys to constructive change

How do effective leaders learn to view change as an opportunity to learn and grow? Quite simply, they build on the five pillars of leadership. More specifically, they:

Key #1—learn to deal constructively with any kind of change.
To do so, leaders must possess clearly defined organizational goals. For leaders and team members, change is often feared because the consequences of change are largely unknown. Achievement in the midst of chaotic, unfamiliar, and changing circumstances is a much more work-intensive process than achievement in ordinary surroundings. A clearly defined program of organizational goals serves to make change less daunting, less threatening, and more manageable, all because the goals define the changes.

In most cases, of course, the changes seem to define the goals. Change itself is often the master of the organization. It tends to set the course and manage the team effort toward a destination of its own choosing. Possessed of a clearly defined organizational plan of action, highly effective leaders are able to turn the tables on change. The goals define the changes to be made, the direction or course to be followed, and the contribution of each team member to make certain those goals are achieved.

Additionally, organizational goals tend to alleviate fear of change. If for no other reason, this should recommend clearly defined goals to every leader and manager! Organizational goals serve to spell out in detail the benefits that leaders and team members will enjoy as a result of change. And, they help each member of the organization construct a clear mental image of the rewarding conditions that will be established as a result of change.

Key #2—learn to encourage the personal growth of team members. Personal growth and Total Person status are not reserved for some sort of leadership elite. Leaders who involve their team members in a planned process of personal growth actually hasten the process of achieving organizational goals. Team members quickly discover that the easiest path to achieving their own personal goals lies in helping the organization reach its goals.

It's our belief that individuals seldom leave organizations for better pay or better working conditions. Instead, they leave most often because they are dissatisfied with their own personal growth. When team members grow personally and become well-rounded individuals, they generate their own supply of positive attitudes, enthusiasm, and excitement.

Why is this important? Because team members who support themselves through these enabling attitudes also tend to support the organization, and their leaders, and other team members. Simply stated, the team member who is growing personally finds renewed excitement in the work—and that excitement is contagious!

Team members who are "green and growing" develop mental attitudes and work habits that are conducive to change. Team members who are "ripe and rotting" resist change and cling to old, unproductive attitudes and habits. The leader's choice is simple: empower these individuals with the opportunity to grow and develop in every area of life or allow them to waste their potential for happiness and achievement. Leaders who consign their team members to the ranks of the forgotten are always frighteningly susceptible to the destructive effects of negative, unharnessed change.

When children don't get positive attention, they sometimes resort to negative behavior to attract the attention they desire. The same is true in an organization—without positive attention, team members can begin to create negative changes to get the attention and recognition they need. Giving team members challenging assignments and adequate rewards will keep them "green and growing" and keep them focused on the organization's short-range and long-range goals.

Key #3—learn to involve team members in the process. Leaders who effectively manage change are also the ones who strive to involve team members in the process of planning, tracking, and evaluating new circumstances, new situations, and new procedures.

While ordinary leaders develop some kind of "oversight committee" composed of a few team members who are expected to give tacit approval to the process of change, highly effective leaders involve every member of the team. Each individual, after all, has something unique to offer: a different perspective, a different idea, or a different attitude. Great leaders see this uniqueness as a treasure chest and strive to make it an integral element of the process of managing change.

Team member participation gives the individual members of your organization a sense of ownership. This vicarious ownership serves to encourage a deeper commitment to the overall success of any organization. Indeed, team member contributions bring loyalty, involvement, and personal commitment that bonds team members to the organization for the long term. Ownership helps reduce the implicit threat of change because it works to make available every team member's intimate knowledge of organizational problems and potential.

A safety net?

The best leaders are always fully aware that team members may not always be as certain of the outcome of change as are the leaders themselves. That's why, when asking their people to change, they are careful to provide some sort of safety net.

A safety net, while it can take many forms, serves only one purpose: it is a provision for handling unexpected obstacles, roadblocks, and other adversities. The provisions of any safety net are based on positive support, such as specific feedback, open communication, and the increased involvement of the leaders themselves.

Of course, team members strive for security—they want to know that they will be able to fulfill their own needs and the needs of their families. No safety net provides that kind of ironclad assurance; the value of a safety net is largely mental rather than financial. Confronted with change and crisis, many leaders retreat into obscurity and silence. They pretend that problems do not exist, even though most members of the organization can see the symptoms develop. As a result, team members become nervous and uneasy—hardly healthy habits of thought for maximum productivity.

In contrast, team members are reassured and will frequently redouble their efforts when they feel that leaders are making an honest effort to communicate challenges and are putting forth the time and effort required to stem the tide of negative change.

People resist change for two reasons. First, change is uncomfortable, and second, change threatens the status quo. When leaders ask their team members to change, they must keep in mind that the natural tendency is exactly the opposite!

Confronting problems and difficulties

Highly effective leaders plan to handle change-related problems. There are, of course, some specific action tools leaders can use in the face of change-induced challenges and difficulties.

It goes almost without saying that a comprehensive goals program will do more to anticipate roadblocks and problems than any other tool. This is because an integral element of such a plan involves the design of a pathway around the problems and hardships that are likely to develop. This goals program can become a catalyst for carefully created procedures that effectively handle problems before they can cause damage to the organization.

Some leaders choose to avoid this sort of pre-problem planning, opting instead to allow any problems that arise to take care of themselves. This is a huge mistake...and a deadly trap. Effective leaders avoid procrastinating in problem situations and they communicate with their team members in an effort to encourage the participation of others and to take advantage of their combined creativity.

As a leader, you may already realize that while you can choose to embrace some change, some change will also be thrust upon you. In either case, you will find that you are able to successfully manage change by making workable plans, implementing your designs, and carefully monitoring progress.

When the space shuttle leaves Earth, great concern focuses on the spacecraft as it builds up maximum aerodynamic pressure just seconds after launch. Effective leaders demonstrate their greatest concern and management efforts as their organization passes through the area of maximum change. By carefully monitoring progress and growth, the pressure of change is reduced to a measurable, manageable level.

An important term, "negative capability," coined by poet John Keats, applies to this important time. Negative capability, Keats defined, is the capability to withstand uncertainties, mysteries, and doubts without irritable reaching after fact or reason.

In other words, negative capability is the ability to bounce back from failure, to overcome obstacles, and to take a calculated risk. You waste not a second in doubt, frustration, or wondering why you're facing obstacles. Obstacles are a fact of life.

Singapore businessman Y. Y. Wong put it best when he said, "Negative capability allows you to refuse to let the negative forces in your environment control you and your emotions."

The option of restructuring

The last few years have seen organizational restructuring emerge as a quick fix for change-induced problems. This restructuring is indeed a viable method of dealing with the effects of change and can be carried out on several different levels: leaders can restructure the entire organization or just revamp the assignment of responsibilities. But either way, effective restructuring is no quick fix.

To make restructuring acceptable to team members, leaders must begin by making careful plans. Those plans first involve the organization's goals program. Leaders who lack clearly defined organizational goals usually use restructuring as a stop-gap measure, hoping to delay the relentless march of change long enough to find something that will permanently stem the tide.

Leaders who have involved their team members in the development of organizational goals are often surprised to find that other individuals recognize the need for restructuring first! Defensive or inflexible attitudes and habits are discarded when team members become an integral part of the goal-setting process; they typically view restructuring as a positive, productive necessity, another step toward the achievement of the organization's ultimate goals. When team members are involved in the process of setting goals, they are also involved in the process of goals achievement. If restructuring aids in that effort, team members will see it as a positive way of moving further down the road to success.

If necessary, changes should be made in the structure of an organization, but gradually. Why? Because leaders and team members find smaller changes easier to assimilate and adjust to than larger changes. However, if the organization's goals program makes a full reorganization an absolute necessity, carrying out the complete restructuring all at once may be preferable to dragging it out. Dragged out long enough, restructuring can result in a serious loss of organizational stability, to say nothing of the loss of your own stability in the process!

Whatever time schedule you choose for your restructuring effort, be sure to involve team members in the planning process. Your key people deserve your reassurance and support; after all, they support and reassure the entire organization. When you present restructuring as an opportunity for improvement, you will find that team members respond with increased productivity, better quality and service, and a new awareness of their opportunity to contribute to both personal and organizational success.

The secret of surviving change

In the final analysis, surviving crisis and change demands one thing of every leader—flexibility. Flexibility is the ability to bend without breaking. It gives you the ability to hold fast to your goals, your mission, and your cause. It enables to separate the means from the end result.

Inflexible leaders lack that delicate balance between maintaining control of the organization and striving to fulfill the needs of team members. Flexible leaders, on the other hand, are keenly sensitive to the needs of the individuals within the organization. They are willing to make minor adjustments in their plan of action to accommodate those needs.

That willingness to make minor adjustments fosters respect among team members. When you are willing to cater to their needs, they willingly follow you and your leadership. In the midst of change, you can depend on them to respond positively as they play their part in the effort to keep the organization on track. Their efforts are conducive to organizational stability—and your flexibility has created their willingness to go the extra mile.

In every arena of life—in families, schools, civic organizations, and in businesses—flexibility is the key to positive and productive change. Flexibility, more than perhaps any other characteristic of highly effective leaders, constructively blends both personal and organizational goals. The end result is committed individuals—team members who are sold out to the achievement of your objectives as well as their own.

How to manage priorities effectively

In times of constant change and challenge, leaders and managers are continually faced with the need to determine priorities. This is another area in which a working goals program makes a valuable contribution. Such a program of organizational objectives helps every member of the team identify what comes first, what comes second, and so on.

The action steps for achieving specific organizational goals serve to determine which part of the effort will be yours and what work will be given to other members of your team. We believe that the most effective way of choosing your own activities is that of determining the time cost involved for you.

Based on your annual income and the number of hours you work per week, it is possible to determine with a fair degree of accuracy what you are being paid for each week, each day, and each hour on the job. When you realize what your time is actually worth in terms of dollars and cents, it becomes far easier to choose the items you will perform personally and those you will delegate to others in the organization.

This comparing the cost of your time with the worth of the activity involved is an effective way to set both personal and organizational priorities. You should not squander a good deal of your valuable time on projects that can be handled by those whose time costs your organization less money.

Some leaders choose to establish priorities by evaluating the contribution each specific activity will make to the achievement of the team's overall goals. Obviously, activities that help move you and your organization closer to predetermined objectives demand a higher priority than those that will produce little real benefit. Any leader's time is best spent on items that produce the highest rate of financial return for the organization. If time is left over, it can be applied to activities that are lower in priority.

The value of an hour

When you know the dollar value of each hour of your working time, you can couple that figure with the value of the activity itself and the contribution the activity will make to overall organizational goals. You should also have a good idea of the amount of time the activity will consume. Then you are ready to choose a particular strategy for handling that activity—or to decide whether it should be handled at all!

Some activities, of course, are essential to the smooth operation of the organization. Yet the level of skill needed to accomplish them is often so low that you should not spend your time on that activity. Instead, find someone on your team to whom you can delegate the activity. If that individual's time costs your company less than your own time, you've just made an additional profit.

> **Effective leaders have learned to delegate low-cost items, routine activities, and anything that can be done by someone else without personal attention and intervention on the part of the leader.**

Moreover, you have helped a member of your team grow and improve. As if that weren't enough benefit, delegation goes a long way toward establishing clear priorities and values for the balance of the team.

Many leaders fail to develop a clear understanding of priorities because they have failed to create adequate job descriptions for other

133

members of the team. In this case, team members have little or no idea of what they should be doing with their time. The notion of establishing priorities for themselves and other people is typically an exercise in abstract thinking. Full job descriptions, on the other hand, give leaders a clear picture of the work flow and how assignments are handled.

Effective leaders look for items of work that can be rearranged quickly and efficiently. These are typically items that are related to each other and things that might be done more quickly and easily by one person than by several team members. It is, of course, the leader's responsibility to make sure that each activity item is actually completed by the team member who can do it most quickly and most accurately.

Priorities help leaders spot those items or activities that should be eliminated altogether. These are items that provide so little contribution to overall organizational goals that the time to perform them is not a justifiable expense. The best leaders are often those who are willing—even eager, in some cases—to do away with reports, activities, and rituals that have managed to survive long enough to outlive their usefulness.

Keeping in touch with the changing organization

Along with planning ahead and establishing priorities, staying informed is a critical attribute for effective leaders who embrace organizational change. While tedious and time-consuming to establish, a system for handling each part of the day-to-day routine cuts down on the number of decisions that must be made by leaders and managers. Additionally, a system helps transform problems into automatic procedures and ensures that the individual most qualified will handle a given situation when it arises.

Effective leaders eliminate a great deal of the anxiety that typically accompanies change when they already have four key elements in place:

#1—clearly defined procedures that govern all routine functions within the organization. This is where an up-to-date procedures manual comes into play. Such a manual helps to train new team mem-

bers and to keep everyone on track toward completion of a specified activity. Additionally, clearly defined procedures help reduce time that might otherwise be used in giving instructions. They also help eliminate repetitive decision-making and prevent the accidental omission of important activities.

#2—regular reports requested on a monthly basis (if not more frequently) from each team member in a position of leadership or management. The report should deal with items that are clearly linked to the achievement of specific organizational goals. To help team members engage in the planning process at their level, monthly reports should focus on accomplishments during the previous month, current problems and plans for solving them, and detailed plans for accomplishment in the month ahead.

#3—the availability and accessibility of the leaders. Seldom do highly effective leaders lead on an absentee basis. They know that they must be available and accessible to provide direction, coaching, and encouragement to each member of the organization. A leader's accessibility has a profound effect on the attitude of the organization. Your accessibility, both physical and emotional, provides team members with the confidence to move forward.

#4—being a good listener and a keen observer of people and events. These leaders have learned to relate what they have observed to the organization's overall goals. Additionally, their skill enables them to pick up hints of trouble before some serious difficulty actually develops and to stay informed and abreast of change within their organization. In this way, they are equipped to respond effectively to the challenge of change and to act creatively to produce solutions that will improve the productivity of the entire team.

Can stress work for you?

The stressless leader is a perpetuated myth. The fact is every leader and manager, in any facet of any organization, experiences some level of stress. The most effective leaders, however, develop their skills for using stress as a force for achievement rather than a destructive entity.

When does stress strike most leaders? Typically, stress occurs when conditions produce an awareness that some action is needed to solve a problem, satisfy a particular need, or prevent some negative result. When leaders believe that the pressure to act can be met by calculated and well-defined action, stress is a constructive agent. But if the perceived need requires more time, greater skill, or more money, stress can become a destructive force.

Stress is evident physically and psychologically, sometimes both at the same time. Primitive emotions, activated and encouraged by stress, cause leaders and followers to rise up to meet a perceived threat. Body functions speed up—the muscles are stimulated and prepared for extraordinary effort. If some sort of strenuous physical activity follows this physical preparation, the body returns to normal just as soon as the need or threat has been met.

If, however, the perceived threat isn't eliminated by the body's activity, the physical preparation continues...and continues...and continues. The body keeps on preparing itself to meet a threat. Often, exhaustion sets in before the threat is eliminated.

Dealing with stress isn't an easy task for many leaders. They take antacids to ease stomach discomfort and swallow painkillers to alleviate back pain. And these are just the beginning; all sorts of physical ailments plague individuals who live in a constant state of stress.

The psychological effects are even more damaging. Short tempers and frayed nerves are the outward signs of chronic stress that refuses to be satisfied by a reasonable amount of activity. But the greatest damage is done within, to attitude and spirit. Constant stress destroys the thrill and excitement of achievement because no result seems good enough. Continual stress robs work of its pure joy.

The toll continues to mount. Stress-induced dissatisfaction with personal activity and individual productivity leads to a breakdown in relationships between people at home and at work. Undue stress hampers decision-making effectiveness, decreases individual productivity, and effectively blocks mental creativity.

Stress and change—an invitation to greatness

Stress is often the result of change, and change is often a result of stress. In this circle, both are opportunities and positive challenges, but neither enjoy great popularity. But without stress, motivation withers and dies. Stress and change are essential elements in the order of life.

Effective leaders handle stress in much the same way that they handle change—they look for the positive aspects rather than dwell on the negative effects. Stress, at its core, is a challenge to any leader's creativity. It is a welcome opportunity to showcase leadership performance. Great leaders understand this opportunity and seize it. Winston Churchill's talk of "blood, tears, toil, and sweat" was the rallying cry for Britain in the darkest days of World War II.

Why would stress-induced metaphors serve to motivate you and your team members? Simply stated, your language and behavior reflect your attitude that stress is a challenge and an opportunity. Used in this positive way, stress and change inspire people in every organization to act, to achieve, and to dig deep for the best within themselves.

How to handle leadership burnout

Many business leaders talk about burnout as if it were a living, breathing thing. Actually, burnout is a condition brought about by unrelieved work stress that results in a high degree of emotional exhaustion. Of course, personal productivity is dramatically decreased as well.

The best leaders understand that preventing burnout among team members is just as vital a concern as preventing burnout within themselves. Indeed, leaders

> **"Unless you take change by the hand, it will take you by the throat."**
> —*Winston S. Churchill*

become critical role models as they demonstrate the way in which they constructively manage change and stress to prevent burnout in their own lives.

Effective leaders strive to identify specific causes of stress, then they plan and carry out equally specific actions to minimize or eliminate the causes altogether. Common causes of burnout inducing stress might include work overload, excessive demands on time, unrealistic expectations, and interpersonal conflicts.

Leaders who strive to involve their team members in goal setting exercises for their particular positions find that the levels of uncertainty and conflict are considerably reduced. Uncertainty fades away in the presence of a plan of action and clearly defined goals and role conflicts decline when team members have a clear definition of their own responsibilities.

Showing team members genuine care and concern goes a long way to eliminate stress within the organization. Successful leaders are always engaged in information gathering conversations that will provide them with the information necessary to cope with pressure, change, and performance expectations.

Effective leaders know that the more control team members exert over their own lives, the more likely the team members are to achieving their own personal goals—and the more inclined they are to put forth the effort necessary to achieve company goals. Let stress and change inspire you to become more sensitive to the needs of your team members. While you inspire other members of the organization to remain productive and to achieve specific performance goals, you become more skillful in managing stress, change, and preventing burnout.

> **In the quest to manage change, you cannot forget to continue working to change yourself.**

Keeping your perspective in the midst of change

Why are you doing what you're doing? Presumably, you and your team members develop plans of action in all six areas of life for the express purpose of reducing stress, planning for change, eliminating old habits and attitudes, and enhancing your enjoyment of life. But when the going gets tough, you will find yourself asking this same question again and again.

The answer happens to be in six parts—one for each area of life:

1) Financial & Career

In the financial and career aspect of your own life, strive to exercise the same careful watch over your personal finances as you do for your organization. Don't lose sight of your career goals—they are guideposts that you can cling to for support when the blizzards of change assail you. This area of life is critical to your continued success. It provides you with the income, the influence, and the sense of accomplishment that helps you achieve goals in the other five areas.

2) Physical & Health

In terms of your personal physical and health area, you can weaken the effects of stress and change by adding a sensible diet, a good exercise program, and adequate rest. Your body is the support structure for your active and creative mind.

3) Family & Home

In the family and home area of life, you can apply some of the time and energy you've saved through crystallized thinking and specific goal-management at work. Strive to maintain worthwhile relationships with every member of your family. You will find it easy to demonstrate the same care and concern for them as you have for your team members.

4) Mental & Educational

The mental and educational area offers you continued opportunities to grow in knowledge of your career field and other areas of interest. Stimulate yourself to think and ponder important ideas by making a point of reading something new each day.

5) Spiritual & Ethical

The spiritual and ethical area of your life also demands attention. Work to become the kind of person you want to be—someone who supports the values you want to demonstrate to others. You have an opportunity to give back to others some of the blessings and rewards that have been given to you. Don't fail to do just that! Search for a cause greater than yourself—some worthwhile endeavor that you can support with your time, effort, and money.

6) Social & Cultural

Many leaders find that the social and cultural relationships they develop in that area of life extend no further than the company doors. Invoke change to help yourself develop a wider circle of friends with whom you share mutual interests.

Growth means change

While you may be assaulted and confronted by the forces of change and stress on a daily basis, you cannot afford to neglect your own personal and professional growth. By now, you've grasped the important dynamics of that growth in your own life. The same dynamics apply to growth within your team members and within your organization.

The bottom line is always the same: growth means change. If you fail to change, you fail to grow. If you fail to help your team members change, they fail to grow. If you and your team members fail to move forward through change, your organization doesn't just remain stagnant—it begins a downward spiral toward oblivion. For yourself and your organization, the process of planning growth takes on paramount importance. The old saying, "Fail to plan, plan to fail," is literally true. The key to managing per-

> **"I am convinced that if the rate of change inside an organization is less than the rate of change outside, the end is in sight."**
> —*Jack Welch*

sonal and organizational change lies in the acquired ability to crystallize and clearly define the future. Leaders who possess and utilize this ability bridge the leadership gap by moving across the five pillars of leadership to the higher ground of greater accomplishment.

Chapter Ten

How to Bridge
the Leadership Gap

Within each person lies the potential to become far more than they are. That expectation—the development of human potential for success and achievement—is best realized through effective leadership.

As you develop the five pillars of leadership to bridge the leadership gap, you may gain a deeper appreciation for the responsibility of leadership. After all, no one really has more power to influence team members and to directly affect their level of productivity than you do. The responsibility becomes even weightier when you realize that, to your team members, *you* are the organization they serve.

YOU are the organization

Why do team members typically possess this singularly narrow view? Because while you may or may not run the entire organization, you do at least run their part of it. You encounter daily opportunities to arrive at decisions, determine schedules, recommend or offer promotions and raises, establish or alter procedures, and provide your team members with other news and information.

Middle managers wear yet another hat. They must do their job with confidence, while at the same time have the respect and trust of both the rank-and-file and the upper management of the organization

Leaders who run the organization, on the other hand, find that success is a balancing act. They are required to balance the potential

143

and desire of the work force against the typically ponderous requirements of the business.

Wherever you may find yourself, the leadership spectrum
exerts unique and unrelenting demands. You'll find that a continuing
program of training and personal development is a key to securing the
confidence and trust of your team members and to ensuring the overall
success of the organization. All training has but one goal: to develop a
more productive and more versatile work force.

Personal development, on the other hand, inspires team members to take greater pride in themselves and in their potential for
achievement. While personal development often expresses itself in
intangible ways—like an enhanced spirit of cooperation and a greater
sense of pride—it creates valuable benefits when coupled with training.
The result of training and personal development is a combined reduc-
tion in costs and an increase in quality, productivity, and overall performance.

The point is that training and personal development typically
produce few benefits when applied independently. Workers may gain
greater satisfaction from the work they do, but if they are still dissatisfied with themselves, the work will still suffer. Conversely, workers may
feel excited about who they are and where they are going in life, but
without specific skill-building and job related training, they may
become frustrated at their inability to climb the ladder to greater success.

The importance of team development

Our team members are often asked, "What one attitude should
leaders and managers change to enhance overall effectiveness?" They
always reply that leaders and managers should *give up the notion that
training and personal development are luxuries.*

Effective leaders who are genuinely concerned with team member efficiency, productivity, and happiness, realize that training and
personal development are absolute necessities.

Some leaders, of course, work to avoid training team members
because they fear that eventually a team member will replace them at

the helm of the organization. You should choose to look on this possibility as an incredible benefit. If you have no one prepared to take your place, you are destined to stay just where you are! Even managers avoid training because they believe trainees will advance past them.

Leaders and managers who feel plagued by insecurity and fear of training should remember that they have not yet reached the ultimate limit for earnings and advancement. There are always opportunities to expand individual contribution to an organization. Sometimes, discovering the opportunity requires patient searching, but it is always

> **"What lies behind us and what lies before us are tiny matters compared to what lies within us."**
> —*Ralph Waldo Emerson*

there. There is no real reason for a leader or manager to expect that the organizational ladder offers no higher rung to climb. If you want to move up the organizational ladder, develop others to take your place. Your job is not to perpetuate the status quo; your job is to teach, coach, and encourage team members to develop their innate potential for achievement.

Many leaders and managers believe themselves too busy to take time to train and develop their team members or themselves! The truth is that training yourself and your organization is an ongoing responsibility. It stands to reason that the busier you are, the more important it is to gain new skills and impart them to your team members. The freedom to do your job better carries a price tag: the cost is measured in effective training and development of your team members.

You are a role model

You will find that the attitudes of your team members toward training and performance improvement *mirror your own attitudes*. How do you feel about innovation? About change? About improvement? How do you communicate your own estimate of their potential and the value of the work they do?

In the final analysis, your attitudes establish the prevailing atmosphere of thought for your team members, your habits of thought determine how receptive team members will be to the pursuit of excellence, and your commitment to personal and professional development determines how seriously team members approach both individual and on-the-job improvement. It's as simple as that.

Managing your attitudes toward your team members and personal growth is the litmus test of effective leadership. If you are successful, you reap rewards in 3 areas:

Improved productivity: Productivity improves because people improve; when they feel better about themselves and the job they are doing, team members follow the natural order of progress and growth just like everyone else.

Enhanced interpersonal relationships: Team members are flesh and blood, just like you. As your workers continue to grow and improve, you develop a keen personal interest in their progress. The result is a closer relationship than ever before; your co-workers become your colleagues and, ultimately, your friends.

Better morale, better attitudes: When team members are growing personally and feeling better about themselves, the morale of the organization improves by a process of osmosis. One individual's positive attitude literally infects another...and so on. The dull, uncaring attitude that may have characterized your team members is quickly replaced by a positive, vibrant view of the organization and the contribution it makes to society.

How to attract a team

People join your team and become members of your organization when both the team and the organization promise to meet the person's basic individual needs. As long as that promise is kept, team members tend to stay. If the promise is somehow broken or ignored, they may leave in a hurry!

In finding and keeping team members who are committed to excellence, leaders should recognize the law of attraction—that dynamic organizations attract dynamic team members. A work environment that stimulates creativity and makes the work experience a reward instead of a chore typically attracts individuals who are seeking the opportunity to contribute and to grow personally.

Of course, the organization's climate hinges on the attitudes, examples, and goals of the leader. The best leaders carefully design and nurture an atmosphere of positive attitudes, trust, and cooperation. This atmosphere, in turn, nurtures continuous individual improvement and productivity. In a word, such an atmosphere makes creativity and success acceptable.

The foundation of this successful climate is composed of clear expectations. Crystallized thinking and well-laid plans provide a strong and steady platform upon which to build organizational climate. But clear expectations also must form integral parts of the structure. Indeed, they become the walls within which the positive and growth-oriented climate is created.

How? Take job descriptions, for example. Well-written job descriptions serve to outline responsibilities, authority for decision-making, and other expected activity. Team members, however, should be encouraged to participate in defining their own jobs. They should not just be handed a featureless job description and told to follow it.

Why? Because no two people ever function the same way, even when placed in exactly the same position. New team members should be allowed the creative freedom to shape and define their job to fit their individual talents and abilities. Leaders may even want to reconstruct different aspects of the organization so that, over time, the strengths and interests of all team members are fully utilized. These kinds of changes bring growth and advancement—and they typically increase productivity as well.

Effective leaders work to supplement sterile job descriptions with one-on-one discussions that give team members an opportunity to ask questions, offer suggestions, and negotiate adjustments that would help them be more productive. However, the leader cannot abdicate the responsibility of clarifying his or her expectations for team members.

147

Likewise, leaders should let team members know what to expect from them in the way of resources, advice, support, and counsel.

Your job as a leader is to provide realistic expectations and acceptable standards of excellence. As you strive for clarity in your expectations, you will find that frustration is minimized, team members experience greater work satisfaction, and a deep sense of accomplishment, and other quality individuals will be attracted to your team.

How to keep a team

People want to work in an environment that offers the opportunity to grow in both skill and responsibility. This fundamental truth gives leaders another important responsibility: when delegating, leaders need to give team members the authority and resources required to complete the assignment. Leaders who hand out assignments without providing support undermine—if inadvertently—the credibility and motivation of their team members.

Highly effective leaders always seek ways to enhance the credibility of their team members. If someone is missing goals or making poor decisions, the best leaders choose to coach rather than criticize. Situations that impair productivity are actually opportunities in disguise—opportunities to teach a better way, to stimulate or improve critical thought, and to create even more effective procedures.

When you take advantage of negative situations by making them opportunities for growth, your team members develop and build their own competency. Their loyalty to you and their bond with the organization become stronger and your authority is enhanced.

Tapping into the entrepreneurs around you

Effective leaders are always on the lookout for ways to make use of the entrepreneurial tendencies among team members. Of course, the entrepreneurial spirit is critically important, but if every individual started his or her own business, there would be no one available to help run them!

Creative leaders understand that giving team members ownership of their work will attract and keep good people. Leaders who make the best use of team member creativity, initiative, and the quest for individual achievement are faced less often with replacing a member of the organization who has left for greener pastures.

Leadership pitfalls to avoid

Busy leaders and managers with a strong achievement drive can sometimes fall into what might be called a "leadership pitfall" that severely limits their potential success and even destroys individual creativity. Only when effective leaders are aware of these pitfalls can they take the positive actions necessary to avoid them.

• *Doing Too Much:* The failure to delegate properly tends to trap unsuspecting leaders and managers under the pressure of too much paperwork, too many details to handle, and too little time for creative planning and management. Essentially, the leader's attitude is the culprit. Leaders who believe in their people, train them well, and give them the opportunity to accept responsibility for significant projects avoid this problem altogether.

• *Doing Too Little:* Just as crippled and devastated as the leader who fails to delegate is the leader who over-delegates. Before giving authority and responsibility to team members, leaders must assure themselves that those individuals have been adequately trained, have "bought into" common goals, and are not already overburdened beyond their potential. Not doing enough research results in an out-of-touch leader—someone who has lost control of the organization. Such a leader can no longer influence organizational direction.

An effective leader avoids this pitfall by keeping an up-to-date, written plan for delegating, along with an implementation schedule and details of what is to be delegated and to whom.

• *Failing to Recognize Personal Growth Needs:* In their concern for helping team members grow and improve, leaders may tend to neglect their own personal growth needs. Effective leaders never assume that they have learned all they need to learn, developed all the skills required for their continued success, or have become all that their potential allows. Any leader, regardless of status or stature, still has more potential for success available for immediate use. A plan of action for personal growth, coupled with decisive action toward goals in all six areas of life, will ensure adequate recognition of the leader's own need for personal growth.

• *Acceptance of Mediocre Performance:* All leaders learn that continual striving for excellence is, in and of itself, hard work.That's why many leaders and managers make the mistake of accepting mediocre performance from their team members and from themselves as well. What is "average" performance cannot be magically transformed into "good enough" for the leader or follower who aspires to real success and achievement.

Highly effective leaders carry but one standard—excellence. They demand outstanding results from themselves and all those who are associated with them. They continually monitor progress toward organizational goals, comparing current results to those obtained last month, last quarter, and last year. Then, they push for greater improvement.

• *Failure to Use Team Member Potential:* Many leaders find it easy enough to drift along, allowing their team members to do the same work they've always done. But it is a mistake to assume that past performance is a reliable indicator of how much your team members can really do. Effective leaders study their people; they learn team member strengths, desires, and personal goals. Leaders can then give team members the opportunity to develop new talents and abilities and to make maximum use of skills already acquired. The best leaders offer team members the chance to acquire new ideas that will help them become more valuable to the organization and more personally fulfilled. When team members grow, the entire organization benefits.

• *Guarding the Status Quo:* When using and applying their valuable past experiences, many leaders cling to what works. "If it ain't broke, don't fix it," is their mantra. An important trap to avoid, however, is the subtle irrationality that forces a leader to maintain the status quo at the expense of losing the organization's cutting edge. Determining the right amount of change for you and your team is a delicate decision. On one end of the continuum is the status quo. At the other end is chaos. Highly effective leaders do not have the luxury of concentrating on only one end of this change continuum. Instead, they must attend to both ends—preserving the core *and* pioneering new territory. As you push the team and yourself to change and grow, yet keep your focus on the unique vision and mission of your company's past and future, your leadership bridge will lead to exciting and profitable territory.

Work hard to preserve your organization's core, yet at the same time pursue ambitious goals for growth and change. As you exercise your personal courage to initiate, inspire, and push for changes that will make your team even more competitive and effectively communicate to your team members why these changes will be worthwhile, they will begin to grow and change with you. They will reflect your excitement and enthusiasm for the work. And they have the security of knowing that you are not implementing change for the sake of change. They know you are furthering the core mission and ideals of your company.

• *Ignoring Problems and Postponing Solutions:* Effective leaders recognize that there is but one time to solve problems—before they occur! The most successful organizational goals programs anticipate potential roadblocks and incorporate plans for overcoming barriers if they do occur. Clear procedures, carefully designed, serve to prevent problems or provide for their properly handling. Crises are thus reduced to something akin to routine events.

When problems occur, the best leaders handle them quickly. Complex problems may require extensive research or planning in order to reach the correct solution. But once a solution has been found, it should be implemented as quickly as possible. The temptation to wait until the problem has solved itself is nothing short of a deadly trap.

This is because of the method in which problems solve themselves. Quite often, leaders and managers who procrastinate when problem solving discover that the problem is destroying the entire organization. This is an incredible waste. The problem might have been quickly solved using the combined creativity of team members and leaders.

• *Incomplete Communication:* It stands to reason that leaders and managers who encounter difficulty in effective delegation may also have trouble giving team members all the information they need. Other leaders may delegate but make the mistake of assuming that their employees already know everything necessary to complete the assigned task. Incomplete communication often results when leaders and managers fail to listen and creatively interpret the information and feedback offered by others. The best leaders are sound communicators who tend to monitor the communication pulse or climate within their organization.

Incomplete communication may be the most visible sign of a leadership gap. Until effective leaders help close the gap through empowering team members and helping them grow and improve, antiquated leadership and management styles will never really change.

The benefits of bridging the leadership gap

Developing your full potential as an effective leader involves an incredible amount of hard work. This is as it should be. Any kind of personal growth always requires effort, and developing your leadership skill is no exception. You may find that you achieve some leadership goals fairly quickly with only a small investment of time, effort, and money.

More significant leadership goals, however, may take a number of years to complete and may require nearly endless amounts of time and hard work on your part. But everything worth having—including the status of highly effective leadership—carries a unique price tag. Just as every worthwhile goal produces significant rewards, so your leadership success is equally rich in benefit for yourself and others.

The most evident returns on your investment in effective leadership are your position and financial rewards. These tangible benefits enable you to fulfill more basic needs and give you the freedom to devote time and attention to higher levels of needs and personal growth.

Additionally, leadership success earns you the respect and trust of your team members as well as others outside the organization. As they follow you, your team members encourage you to become even more competent and more successful. You will find that other members of the community share their respect and trust for you. In this way, you begin to exert a leadership influence that goes far beyond the somewhat limiting scope of the organization. Additionally, you find new and exciting opportunities for personal growth and service to others.

Your own awareness of your professional competence is a prime reward of your growth as an effective leader. For someone who is self-motivated and goal directed, that sense of personal competence is far more satisfying as a reward than the more tangible rewards that others seem to crave.

Your leadership competence shows that you possess a lofty and noble desire—the desire to attain some measure of lasting achievement and to contribute something to the lives of other people.

Developing your leadership expertise enables you to reach significant personal goals. Professional success provides you with an income adequate for the necessities of life and for luxuries as well. You find the freedom to structure and manage your own activities and you gain the ability to move in and among any social circle or professional organizations that interests you. Goals in other areas of life become more attainable as you continue to grow professionally and personally.

The most exciting reward

At the core of leadership success lies the most exciting reward of all: the ability to offer new opportunities to other people. Your team members become like family and you:

- feel the same intense desire to help them grow and achieve their own personal goals

- find joy in helping your team members achieve their own personal goals and find satisfaction in their successes
- share their excitement as you reward their achievement with money, position, and other recognition

Knowing that you have made a direct contribution to the growth of the individuals on your team creates a unique sense of fulfillment—a fulfillment that probably cannot be found any other way.

Your leadership success also enables you to serve your community at large. As an effective leader, you have the skills required to contribute to the management and success of the various groups to which you belong—civic organizations, professional groups, religious and charitable organizations, and so on. Successful leadership is a magnet—it makes people seek you out and ask for your help. In this way, more than any other, you can expand your influence and heighten your impact on other people. This "being of service" adds rich meaning and purpose to your life.

It probably goes without saying that leadership and management growth carries with it abundant financial rewards. How will you use these rewards? Will you see yourself as their rightful owner, with no further thought than your own interests? Or will you see yourself as a temporary steward of these assets, charged with empowering them to do the most good?

Encourage yourself and your colleagues to use the financial rewards of leadership to develop an enjoyment of giving. While we live in a world of abundance, it is an unfortunate fact that not everyone is able to enjoy the abundance. See your financial success as a vehicle that makes possible a college education for a deserving youngster, a badly needed operation for someone in need, or the solution to a housing problem that has burdened your community for decades.

> **"Life is a promise. Fulfill it."**
> —*Mother Teresa*

If helping your team members grow and improve helps you know greater joy, you will also enjoy the immense satisfaction that comes from widening your circle of influence. Extend your efforts as far as possible—strive to give something back to your own community, your society, your nation, and the entire world. You will not regret the experience!

John F. Kennedy once said that "One person can make a difference, and everyone should try." The fact that comparatively few individuals really make a difference in this world attests to the rarity of true givers among us, while takers are abundant.

Being a giver is truly a mark of high calling and a natural calling for any effective leader who bridges the leadership gap.

Conclusion

Every leader has options and choices. Effective leaders possess the responsibility of deciding which options they want to pursue. While many people react with utter confusion when confronted by the challenges and choices of life, great achievers and great leaders respond with confidence and certainty.

But many leaders seem hesitant to make decisions. They seem to genuinely fear commitment to one course of action or another. You may find that you are tempted to try to navigate the choppy seas of indecision by deciding not to decide...anything.

For indecisive leaders, the end result is rather depressing: they achieve little in their lives and for their organizations, especially compared to their vast, untapped potential for achievement. Their failure to accomplish worthy goals can be blamed on their failure to decide what to accomplish.

For leaders and followers, a simple solution to this dilemma exists: ***all of us must, at some point, decide to decide.*** No one can offer only a half-hearted commitment to any of life's choices and challenges if they expect to master it and emerge a truly better person. Effective leaders strive to determine their objectives and focus on them with the zeal of a crusader. They understand that only complete and total commitment to achieving a goal ensures a successful undertaking.

Requirement for achievement

No one can be truly successful without crystallized thinking (leadership pillar #1) and a concise plan for achievement (leadership pillar #2). That is what makes a Personal Plan of Action so important, and that is why a Personal Plan of Action is contained in every Paul J. Meyer program. Using this Plan of Action is the simplest, most effective way to identify, clarify, and plan for the achievement of Total Person goals and objectives.

A Paul J. Meyer program incorporates the best in personal development thinking, offers proven application, makes you think, and guides you step-by-step through the Total Person process. It gives you and your team members the opportunity to create a random list of things you'd like to see happen in each area of life.

Your Plan of Action moves through the development of values and priorities and offers point-by-point coaching through the thinking process necessary to plan for the achievement of important goals. By backing that plan with affirmations and visualization—two important tools for greater success and achievement—our clients develop the vehicle that will guide them to the success they desire.

There is no magic in a Paul J. Meyer program. Sitting on a bookshelf, the program cannot cause anyone to be successful. Each program requires personal involvement, and that involvement continues as you think through the process, put forth the mental effort, and accept the challenges of success.

The next step

To obtain more information about Paul J. Meyer programs in the United States, call Leadership Management, Inc. at 1-800-568-1241 or email: info@lmi-inc.com. We'll introduce you to an LMI affiliate partner who will work with you to understand your unique situation. This individual will then be able to suggest a Paul J. Meyer program that will help you and your team members achieve the objectives you seek.

Outside of the U.S., call our international companies, headquartered in Waco, Texas, at 254-776-7551 or email: info@lmi-inc.com. We'll make sure that you get more information on International programs and courses.

Becoming whole again

Helping people become whole again is the essence of what we do. When leaders are not whole personally, they usually fail miserably in their efforts to direct the actions of others. Often, their own lives are destroyed in the process.

The end result we seek, of course, is the sharing of the Total Person concept with those who make your effort work. If you do not personally use the concept yourself, you cannot effectively share it. Trying to make others into something you are not is tantamount to going back to somewhere you have never been.

If you are trying to lead without becoming a Total Person and a highly effective leader, you cannot be certain of your destination or even of the route you'll take. Enlisting the company of others on such an unplanned journey is perilous indeed. For your own sake—and for the sake of those you lead—strive to become what you were intended to be in each area of life.

When you've mastered the process yourself, you can share it with those who follow you. Working individually with your followers, you will begin to build a committed team. When members of the committed team begin to work together in the same way, a committed organization is created. The end result is that you will have changed the world—you will have done something to put people and society together for the benefit of all.

In all the annals of human history, few leaders have ever made a greater contribution.

Appendix 1—questions at the crossroads

These questions are indicators of your progress in your personal efforts to build a leadership bridge. Can you answer all 11 questions with a resounding "Yes!"?

Question One: *Have I crystallized my thinking so that I know where I stand now and where I want to go?*

Question Two: *Are my vision, mission, and purpose clear to me and to my team members?*

Question Three: *Do I have a detailed, written plan to achieve each important personal and organizational goal, and have I set a deadline for their attainment?*

Question Four: *Are my personal goals balanced with the need to help my organization achieve?*

Question Five: *Do my personal goals represent a balance among the six areas of life?*

Question Six: *Do I have a burning desire to achieve the goals I have set for myself?*

Question Seven: *Have I developed within my team members and myself a passion for achieving the success we've envisioned?*

Question Eight: *Do I have supreme confidence in our ability to reach our goal?*

Question Nine: *Do I trust my team members to strive toward success and to continue to develop more of their innate potential for achievement?*

Question Ten: *Have I accepted personal responsibility for the success of my team—and for the achievement of my own personal goals?*

Question Eleven: *Do I possess the iron-willed determination to follow through regardless of circumstances or what others say, think, or do?*

Appendix 2—goals for six areas of life

The key to becoming a Total Person is to set and achieve meaningful goals in all six areas of life. In Chapter Five, we offered some suggested goals for each area.

In the spaces below, you can jot down ideas for goals in each area—goals that are personally meaningful to you and that will motivate you to use more of your full potential.

Goals for the Family Area:

-

-

-

-

-

-

Goals for the Financial Area:

-

-

-

-

-

-

Goals for the Mental Area:

-

-

-

-

-

-

Goals for the Physical Area:

-

-

-

-

-

-

Appendix

Goals for the Social Area:

-

-

-

-

-

-

Goals for the Spiritual Area:

-

-

-

-

-

-

Appendix 3—the question of risk

I, Paul, have lived a lifetime of thinking, planning, and then jumping in—taking a chance—and it has paid off handsomely for me.

People ask about different businesses I have started and how I knew when I had enough information to make an investment in real estate or any other venture. I tell them I always ask myself these questions:

- What are my goals?

- Can I reach my goal without taking a risk?

- What are the benefits to gain if I take this chance?

- What can I lose by taking a chance—by risking?

- What can I do to prevent these losses?

- Is the potential loss I am thinking about greater than the possible gain?

- Is this the right time to take this action?

- What pressures are on me to make this decision?

- What would I have to know to change my mind about taking this risk?

- What experience do I have taking this type of risk?

- Who is someone I can confide in or ask for advice about this risk?

The Five Pillars of Leadership

- Do I have personal blind spots in my vision about this risk?

- If I take this chance, this risk, will people think more of me or less of me if I succeed? Do I really care?

- If a loss does occur, will I take it personally, or am I able to be realistic and objective about it?

- Will I worry and worry about the risk I have taken?

- Who else has made a similar investment?

- What actions can I take to track my investment and protect it?

- How will this risk affect me, my children, my parents, my friends, my company, and my relationship with my bank?

- Do I really enjoy the lifestyle of an entrepreneur?

Fortunately, anything that has ever happened to me in my role as a leader, salesperson, businessperson, or investor has never affected who I am as a person or reduced my self-image. I make a conscious decision to manage my life to maintain a healthy self-image, peace of mind, and happiness.

A final word by Paul J. Meyer

Years ago, my father copied a poem by Will Allen Dromgoole onto a page of a ruled tablet. I kept the poem for years, folded and tucked into my wallet. Today, it hangs in my office, a reminder of the attitudes and values my parents worked to instill in my brother, my sister, and me.

The poem read:

An old man traveling a lone highway,
Came at evening, cold and gray,
To a chasm deep and wide;
The old man crossed in the twilight dim,
The sullen stream held no fear for him,
But he turned when he reached the other side,
And builded a bridge to span the tide.
Old man, cried a fellow pilgrim near,
You are wasting your strength with your building here,
You never again will pass this way,
Your journey will end with the ending day,
You have crossed the chasm deep and wide,
Why build this bridge at eventide?
But the builder raised his old gray head,
Good friend in the path I have come, he said,
There followeth after me today,
A youth whose feet must pass this way,
This chasm which has been naught to me,
To that fair-headed youth may a pitfall be;
He, too, must cross in the twilight dim,
Good friend, I am building this bridge for him.

August Carl Meyer was a German immigrant. His legacy to his three children—and through us, to the world—has been the foundation for my efforts to help individuals and organizations across the globe build their bridge that will span the leadership gap.

Paul J. Meyer has authored 24 major programs on sales, motivation, goal setting, management, and leadership development with combined sales in 60 countries in 20 languages of more than 2 billion dollars, more than any other author in history. He formed Success Motivation Institute in 1960 and is considered by many to be the founder of the personal development industry.

He is also the founder of Leadership Management, Inc., Success Motivation International, Inc., and nearly 40 other companies spanning the fields of publishing, education, finance, real estate, manufacturing, and more.

His recent books include *I Inherited a Fortune, Chicken Soup for the Golden Soul*, which was on the *New York Times* best-seller list for many months, *Success in Pre-Paid Legal*, and *Unlocking Your Legacy*, which outlines 25 of his top secrets for success.

Paul and his wife Jane have 5 children and 14 grandchildren and live in Waco, Texas.

Randy Slechta is president of the international personal and professional development companies founded by Paul J. Meyer. Under Slechta's direction, Leadership Management International, Inc. and Success Motivation International, Inc. have experienced phenomenal worldwide growth.

A highly sought speaker and trainer, Slechta travels extensively and has spoken in 40 countries to more than a thousand groups on topics ranging from leadership development to personal and professional growth.

Randy, his wife Janna and their three daughters, Morgan, Brooke and Kelsey, reside in Waco, Texas.

For More Information

To obtain more information about Paul J. Meyer programs in the United States, call Leadership Management, Inc. at 1-800-568-1241 or email: info@lmi-inc.com. We'll introduce you to an LMI affiliate partner who will work with you to understand your unique situation. This individual will then be able to suggest a Paul J. Meyer program that will help you and your team members achieve the objectives you seek.

Outside of the U.S., call our international companies, headquartered in Waco, Texas, at 254-776-7551 or email: info@lmi-inc.com. We'll make sure that you get more information on International programs and courses.